KEEPING OUR CHILDREN SAFE

Roberta Cava

Copyright © 2015 by Roberta Cava

All rights reserved. No part of this work covered by the copyrights hereon may be reproduced or used in any form or by any means - graphic, electronic or mechanical, including photocopying, recording, taping or information storage and retrieval systems - without the prior written permission of the publisher.

Published by Cava Consulting

info@dealingwithdifficultpeople.info
www.dealingwithdifficultpeople.info

Cava, Roberta
Keeping Our Children Safe

National Library of Australia
Cataloguing-in-publication data:

ISBN 978-0-9925659-9-2

BOOKS BY ROBERTA CAVA

Non-Fiction

Dealing with Difficult People
(21 publishers – in 16 languages)
Dealing with Difficult Situations – at Work and at Home
Dealing with Difficult Spouses and Children
Dealing with Difficult Relatives and In-Laws
Dealing with Domestic Violence and Child Abuse
Dealing with School Bullying
Dealing with Workplace Bullying
Retirement Village Bullies
Keeping Our Children Safe
What am I going to do with the rest of my life?
Before tying the knot – Questions couples Must ask each other Before they marry!
How Women can advance in business
Survival Skills for Supervisors and Managers
Human Resources at its Best!
Human Resources Policies and Procedures - Australia
Employee Handbook
Easy Come – Hard to go – The Art of Hiring, Disciplining and Firing Employees
Time and Stress – Today's silent killers
Take Command of your Future – Make things Happen
Belly Laughs for All! – Volumes 1 to 4
Wisdom of the World! The happy, sad and wise things in life!

Fiction

That Something Special
Something Missing
Trilogy: Life Gets Complicated
Life Goes On
Life Gets Better

ACKNOWLEDGEMENTS

My thanks go to Marilyn Price-Mitchell, PhD who gave me permission to use her information from *'Disadvantages of Social Networking: Surprising Insights from Teens.'*

I'd also like to thank David Penberthy for allowing me to use his article that was in the Sunday Mail on June 21st, 2015 couriermail.com.au: *'D is for Digital Danger'*

KEEPING OUR CHILDREN SAFE

Table of Contents

Introduction

Chapter 1 – The Dangers of Social Media   1

Cyber harassment
Cyber stalking
Sexual exploitation
Internet safety
Stranger danger
Disadvantages of social networking
    Ten disadvantages of social networking
Addressing the disadvantages of social networking
'D is for Digital Danger'

Chapter 2 – Paedophiles   21

Chat rooms
What is a paedophile?
What causes paedophilia?
Can paedophilia be treated?
Are paedophiles only attracted to children?
One paedophile's story
Paedophiles/child molesters
Hunting predators
Pornography
The dangers of pornography

Chapter 3 – Bullying   33

What is bullying
School bullying
Ignoring the bullying
Signs of bullying

Physical bullies
Verbal bullies
Pornography
Bullies who were targets
Female bullies
Group/exclusion bullies
Those who were excluded
Being excluded may increase the risk of suicide
Exclusion leads to increased aggression
Sexual harassment
Pupil bullying
Bullying of School personnel
Teacher Bullying
Why don't other students help the target?
Helping the target
Is your child a bully?
School Hazing
Stalkers
What parents can do to help a bullied child
Anti-bullying policies
Australian anti-bullying policies

Chapter 4 – Cyber Bullying 63

What is cyber bullying?
Who are the targets of the cyber bullying?
What are the results to the target/target of bullying?
The target's behaviour
The four stages of fear
Examples of cyber bullying
How common is cyber bullying in the teen age years?
Why do people cyber bully?
What can be done about cyber bullying?
Preventing cyber bullying
How you can stop cyber bullying once it starts
Why is cyber bullying serious?
Penalties for cyber bullying

Deal with cyber bullying when it happens
Can cyber bullying be stopped?
Why is cyber bullying so difficult to stop?
When should the police become involved?
How to prevent your child from being targeted

Chapter 5 – New Synthetic Drugs   *83*

Crime Stoppers video on synthetic drugs
What are the new synthetic drugs?
Synthetic cannabis
How can harm from these drugs be reduced?
Smoking during and after pregnancy

Chapter 6 – Illicit Drugs   *91*

Chroming
Alcohol
Analgesics
Benzodiazepines
Caffeine
Cannabis
Cocaine
Ecstacy
GHB
Hallucinogens
Heroin
Inhalants
Methamphetamine
Naloxone
Nitrous oxide
Oxycodone
Synthetic cannabis
Tobacco
Overdose
References
Ice
Murder of Phil Walsh

Chapter 7 – Teen Depression and Suicide   111

Why teens experience moodiness
How to handle normal moodiness
What are mood disorders?
How common are mood disorders?
The difference between moodiness and mood disorders
    Being excluded affects behaviour
How can you tell if your teen is depressed?
What should you do?
Stress breakdown
Self-harm
Who commits suicide?
Factors relevant to teen suicide
    Warning signs
    Treatment
    Talk about it
    Set an appointment with your family doctor
    See a specialist
    Jointly develop a plan
    Continue supporting your teen
What can parents do?
Helping your teen cope with loss
Teen suicide is preventable
Expressing emotional feelings
What causes teenage anger?
    Children's anger – your response
Getting a good night's sleep

Chapter 8 – Growing up   137

Button Batteries
Trust
It's hard being a teenager
Family conferences
Out-of-control teens
Teamwork

Puberty
    Puberty for boys/girls
    Physical changes in boys/girls
    Emotional changes in boys/girls
    Period strategy – think ahead
    Teen girls and self-consciousness
Emotional development and reasoning
Emotional development and romantic feelings

Chapter 9 – Entering Middle School   155

Starting middle school
Discuss changes
How to make the transition easier
Teaching independence to your teen

Conclusion   165

Bibliography   167

Introduction

Since I became a volunteer with Crime Stoppers in Queensland, I've become more and more afraid for our children and grandchildren. In my day, we walked to school on our own, and our parents weren't afraid that paedophiles would bother or abduct us. Now, children hardly go anywhere except in groups or are driven by their parents. What a shame and what a loss of independence this has made to their childhood freedom.

In my day, sure there were drugs, but they were something that I would never see or even have the chance to buy – and I had no interest in them.

There was no social media to keep me from exercising my body. I didn't go to 'chat rooms' and expose myself to paedophiles. I didn't take selfies that I would be ashamed of later when they were splashed over the internet for anyone to see.

There were no mobile phones to keep me texting my friends twenty-four seven. I spoke to my friends – I didn't send them texts or e-mails. I had a life!

A concentrated study needs to be done to determine what's causing our kids to go 'off the rails' to escape from reality by using drugs and viewing pornography at earlier and earlier ages.

On July 15, 2019 the UK will be the first country in the world to demand age verification for people viewing pornography online to verify that they are 18 or over. Porn sites that sell adult content or provide it free will have to employ companies to provide age checks.

Chapter 1
The Dangers of Social Media

Many teens use social networking websites such as Facebook, MySpace, Bebo, Twitter, Linkedin and ProfileHeaven to keep in touch with friends from school, camp, church or work. Teens also use them to strike up conversations with strangers - teenage and otherwise - whether they're seeking help with their homework, advice about a problem or a date for Saturday night.

FaceBook was launched on February 4th, 2004. It was initially meant to be used only by Harvard students, but it soon went viral and is now world-wide. With 1.8 billion users in August 2015 it has been a huge success. However, with so many people having access to this social media, it is no longer safe for individuals to use it to communicate with their friends.

FaceBook and other social media outlets are a godsend for companies and organisations wishing to let the world know about their product or service, but individuals should **not** be using it to communicate with others. For example:

My 15-year-old granddaughter lives in Canada (I live in Australia). She has listed me as one of her 'friends' on FaceBook. I use FaceBook to send my monthly newsletter to over 800 people. I have never met these people – they have subscribed to my newsletter via my website.

If my granddaughter sends me a message and I either click 'like' or send her a message – all 800 of my 'friends' will see her message. If they respond, all their 'friends' will also have access to my granddaughter leaving her open to being approached by a paedophile.

Remember that if they post something and a friend 'likes' or comments on it, their post gets seen by all that person's friends as well. Then someone else comments then all that person's friends see it too. As a result, within minutes of them posting it, their post may be seen by hundreds, even thousands of people they don't even know.

Adults too are in danger by being exposed to identity fraud and stalking by unsavoury people, so they too should not use social media as a method of communicating with their friends.

Children need to be very careful when they go on-line, especially going into chat rooms. Parents can stop their children from going into adult sites but can't stop them from using chat rooms.

One in four children using chat rooms on the Internet will be solicited by a child predator.

Adult *cyber-harassment* or *cyber-stalking* is not cyber bullying. Once adults cyber bully children or try to lure children into offline meetings, it's called *cyber-harassment* or *cyber-stalking.* It is also called *sexual exploitation* or luring by a sexual predator. It's extremely important that children and adults do not give out personal information on Facebook or any of the other internet media sites – better yet – don't go on them at all!

It's extremely important that children and adults do not give out personal information on Facebook or any of the other internet media sites.

Chat rooms are full of paedophiles that prey upon children. For instance, a twelve-year-old girl revealed to her parents that she was corresponding with a fourteen-year-old boy on the internet. He had sent a picture of himself and wanted to meet her at McDonald's. She wondered if she should meet him. Her parents called the police for advice and they arranged to have undercover police officers at the restaurant when she met the boy.

As they suspected, the boy was a grown man, a paedophile, who was arrested at the scene. The man had a prior record and had been jailed for raping two young girls. So, children need to know they should not give strangers any personal information over the internet and should be very cautious about meeting anyone they meet on-line. This man knew where she lived, what school she went to and how old she was.

The police obtained a warrant, searched the man's home, confiscated his computer and learned that he was stalking three other young girls and had already asked them to meet him. The police were able to contact the parents of those girls to warn them about the danger the girls were in.

The police computer experts also examined the information on the girl's computers and were able to catch a paedophile gang who traded information about the young girls.

Paedophiles go on-line to seek tips for getting near children - at camps, through foster care, at community gatherings and at countless other events. They swap stories about day-to-day encounters with minors. And they make use of technology to help take their arguments to others, like sharing on-line printable booklets to be distributed to children that praise the benefits of having sex with adults.

A report of data collected by school authorities in Canada identified that:

- 23% of middle-schoolers surveyed had been contacted by e-mail;
- 35% in chat rooms;
- 41% by text messages on their cell phones.
- Fully 41% did not know the identity of the perpetrators.

So how would children and adults keep in touch with their friends? They would use e-mails where they would send bulk e-mails to the friends they wish to contact. They, of course, could pass on the information, but not in the manner it would be passed on via social media.

Paedophiles don't always use the internet; some may stalk children by following them. Many parents transport their children to and from every event, but some must trust that their children will be safe going to and from school and/or events. These parents should try to arrange (possibly with school assistance) for groups of children who live close by to travel together, hopefully with other older students who can keep an eye out for anyone who looks suspicious. Or parents could share car-pooling to pick up and deliver children.

An excellent book for younger children is ***Benjamin Rabbit and the Stranger Danger*** by Irene Keller.

There are excellent on-line resources for parents:

- ***Cyber Bullying & Grade School-Aged Kids:***
  http://childparenting.about.com/od/technologyentertainment/a/Cyberbullying-And-Grade-School-age-Kids.htm
- ***Internet Safety On-Line:***
  http://childparenting.about.com/od/technologyentertainment/a/Internet-Safety-For-Kids.htm

Internet Safety

These paedophiles seek a target-rich environment for finding their prey and the Internet has become their stalking ground. To ensure that your children and household are safe from the threat of these predators, parents need to know how to protect their children:

- When possible, don't leave your child alone in a room with a computer connected to the Internet. Any Internet-connected computer should be in the community part of the house. It should only be used when parents are home and can monitor their children's

activity on the computer. Think about it like this; would you ever let a stranger go up to your child's bedroom and talk to them alone for four hours? Would you ever leave your child alone in a park and come back four hours later?
- It's a myth that a child on a computer at home is safe. At the least, they may be exposed to sexually explicit materials, and at the worst, they can be lured by an Internet paedophile.
- Parents should educate themselves on basic computer knowledge. They should be the ones who set up all Internet accounts and passwords. Make sure you know your child's account name and password. You should also be aware of any other e-mail accounts your child may have. Take the time to learn about Internet filters, firewalls, monitoring software and other tools. Use your browser history, cache and cookies to find out what sites your children have been visiting. Enter their names, including nicknames, into popular search engines to see if they have public profiles on social networking sites. Do the same with your address and phone number. You might be surprised by how much of your personal information is on-line!
- *Locking certain computer sites doesn't work. Computer filters don't work for chat rooms, and there are no blocks for chat rooms. There is software to monitor a child's activity, but not their chat activity.*
- Be aware. Parents should be cautious if a child suddenly closes a browser window on the computer when the parent enters the room, or if the child doesn't want the parent to see what they're working on. If the parent questions what the child is looking at, they should go to the computer and click the back button on the tool bar or lean over and look closely at the computer screen. Parents should also be aware of pictures coming in over the computer.

- Caution them to never, ever give out personal information over the Internet. This is a good practice for both children and parents. It makes it easy for people to find out about them if they have provided them with any personal information. If they must give some information, only give their state identification. Never give out their city, birthday, name, or school they attend.
- Children should never upload a picture of themselves onto the Internet. They should also never e-mail a picture to this new person. Once the picture leaves their computer, they have lost control of what can be done with the picture. A predator can do anything they want with it. Stop your children from taking and distributing 'selfies.'
- Make sure you have open lines of communication with your children. *Oftentimes children are communicating with strangers because there's no communication in the home.* Have open discussions with your children so they feel comfortable talking with you. They should know that if they receive material that bothers them or if it's inappropriate, they should bring it to your attention, so it can be reported to local law enforcement. They need to feel comfortable doing this.
- Many times, children feel they did something wrong or something they weren't supposed to do, so they think they'll lose computer privileges because of this. It's important for them to know that they can bring it to their parents' attention without getting into trouble.

If you suspect your child is in trouble, look for these signs:
- A child that starts to act differently, withdrawn, getting bad grades or spending a lot of time on the Internet. Many times, children will think they have found their new 'best friend' and they believe that this person will rescue them from their doldrums.

If gifts start arriving at the home, this should also be a clue that something is not right. If your family starts receiving phone calls from people you don't recognise, this could mean there are serious problems. Either the child gave the predator your phone number or the predator found it. This can signify a threat to your child as well as the entire family, especially if the predator knows where you live.
- If you suspect your child could be the target of an Internet paedophile, call your local law enforcement agency immediately.

Stranger Danger

Teach your children about 'stranger danger.' As scary as it may be, parents need to talk to their children about people who might want to hurt them. The best way to protect your children is to get them involved in their own protection:

- Parents need to be aware of possible predators. Typical signs are: someone who seems too good to be true, who offers extensive help to your family, who knows too much about your children or children in general, especially if they don't have children of their own. You should know all the adults who can have contact with your child.
- Talk to your children about paedophiles as soon as they can understand what you mean. As early as three to five years of age. When children begin to interact with the world, they're subject to being targets.
- Tell your child you love them no matter what. Remind them that they can tell you anything and you will still love them with all your heart.
- Don't be afraid that you're scaring your children, but don't ask them to deal with adult issues either. Speak to them in age-appropriate language and give them instructions about what to do. They will feel empowered by knowing how to protect themselves. Be

careful sharing your own experiences if you were a target of sexual molestation for example. Providing too many details and rehashing the tragedy can create a sexually charged environment and be harmful for your children in the long run.

- Children need to know that they have the right to say 'No,' yell, or ask for help. It may contradict what they know about respecting adults, but tell them if they feel threatened, they have your permission to make a scene, or to run away to a public place. And they need to know they won't get into trouble if their fears were unwarranted. Let them know that no one has the right to hurt them or touch them inappropriately. Teach your child to call you if a stranger arrives when there are no other adults around.
- Make sure your children know what acceptable behaviour is and what is out-of-bounds; that there are private areas of their bodies that no one else should touch.
- Rehearse your child's response to danger. If s/he doesn't practice it, your child won't really know what to do. Telling your child to yell for help isn't enough. In the face of danger, a child could forget, so rehearse, role-play and practice what your child should do.
- Remind your children that predators don't necessarily look scary or strange. A dangerous person could look like the person next door, or even be someone they know.

Disadvantages of Social Networking: Surprising Insights from Teens: by Marilyn Price-Mitchell, PhD – Used with Permission.

Marilyn Price-Mitchell, PhD is a developmental psychologist and Fellow at the Fielding Institute for Social Innovation. She writes for *Psychology Today* about positive youth development.

'Honestly, I sometimes truly wish that 'tools' such as the iPhone (or any smartphone) laptops, iPads, tablets, etc. hadn't been invented. Sure, they're great, incredibly useful and fun time-killers, but the way teenagers abuse them and turn them into mini social control rooms is frankly awful.'

At first glance, you might think this quote came from a parent or grandparent lamenting on the disadvantages of social networking and how social media has doomed today's children. However, it was written by a tenth grader as part of an assignment to answer the question, 'How has on-line social networking influenced your relationships with friends and family?'

The student went on to write, *'The teenage way of life has completely changed from what it was only twenty years ago. Now, there's a dramatic decrease in face-to-face communication, which reduces our generation's ability to interact with others on a speaking level.'*

Ten Disadvantages of Social Networking

Here are the most discussed disadvantages of social networking according to these tenth graders, including quotes from their essays.

1. Lacks emotional connection

'A couple of weeks ago, one of my friends and I got into a fight and she told me all of her feelings as to why she ignored me for two weeks. Assuming it would have been hard to say it to my face, she sent me a text message. The negative side was I didn't know if she truly felt sorry because I didn't hear it from her. The quality of a conversation using social media is awful because you cannot sense the emotion or enthusiasm from the other person. It makes you wonder if they actually mean what they say.'

2. Gives people a license to be hurtful

'I do think it has gotten to an extreme point where you can say things you can't say or get away with in person'

'I'm disappointed whenever I hear about social media being used to hurt people. I wonder if this happens when the writers forget that there are real people behind the screen.'

3. Conveys inauthentic expression of feelings

'Social media conversations today are filled with "ha ha" "LOL," and other exclamations that are meant to represent laughter. This shorthand has become second nature and is often used when the sender is not even smiling, much less laughing in real life. According to Robin Dunbar, an evolutionary psychologist at Oxford, the actual physical act of laughter and not the abstract idea of something being funny, is what makes laughing feel so good. If we are so willing to replace the act that, honestly, we all love, with an artificial, typed representation that doesn't even bring the same joy, what else would we be potentially subconsciously, willing to exchange?'

4. Decreases face-to-face communication skills

'Computer reliance could hurt a person's ability to have a face to face conversation by making it awkward and unusual to hear something and respond with a thoughtful message through the spoken word because of one's dependence on a keyboard to convey a message.'

5. Diminishes understanding and thoughtfulness

'Since the inception of social networking, the quality of conversations has dropped. I believe that people are spending so much time on-line that they don't always understand the feeling, emotion and/or character of the person they're talking to. When you talk to someone through a message or even a voice, you can't always fully understand them.'

'Social networking has ruined the thoughtfulness in basically saying hello in person. For instance, you could say hello to your friend in Germany with Facebook, chat in seconds; but what if there was no way to communicate via social networking? Well you would have to write them a letter or phone them and that is something very thoughtful.'

6. Causes face-to-face interactions to feel disconnected

'When I see my friends on their phones and I'm around them, I feel disconnected even though we're only two feet apart... Unfortunately, sometimes friends use their phones so much that it's difficult to have an actual conversation with them. Some friends can get so socially attached to something such as a blog or gaming console that they lose touch with friends, creating small gaps and holes in close friendships/relationships.'

7. Facilitates laziness

'The new socially active era causes laziness because instead of running to your friends, you can message them. Or instead of walking upstairs to notify the family of dinner, I can blog it. Social networking makes life so convenient that it creates laziness. In my opinion staying fit is important, but it's difficult to go beyond the newly developed status quo.'

'It's really easy to spend hours doing nothing... It's a fantastic way to waste time.'

8. Creates a skewed self-image

'We tell ourselves lies about ourselves and develop something we're not. We post pictures of us looking perfect and share the good news. We never post pictures of ourselves when our dog dies, when someone we love leaves and when we lose a job. We never share the bad news that always clouds our lives. We all develop this perfect image

of ourselves and some of us actually try to rely on this imaginative thought we have of ourselves instead of staying true to who we are.'

9. Reduces family closeness

'Texting, Facebook, Twitter and Gmail alienate us from our families more than we actually think it does... When my family is spending family time together and watching a movie my brother and I are on our phones rather than actually watching the movie with our parents.'

10. Causes distractions

'When I have my phone out, it makes me feel like nothing else is going on around me. I use social media as a way to feel popular, important and just to fit in. My friends and I always compare ourselves to each other, wondering who has more Facebook friends or Twitter followers. But what really ends up happening is I begin to talk less and end up relying on text for a conversation. Ever since I got a Smartphone, I have been distracted from everything. I watch television less, do homework less and even spend less time with my friends and family.'

Addressing the Disadvantages of Social Networking

The disadvantages of social networking and social media will continue to be studied for decades to come. In the meantime, we already know it's a significant source of concern among privacy advocates as well as parents who worry about their children's safety. But clearly, the disadvantages of social networking go much deeper than privacy and safety. These high school students described some of the serious drawbacks to relationships – the foundation of human development.

In his book ***Lightweb Darkweb; Three reasons to reform Social Media before it reforms us***, Raffi Cavoukian provides an abundance of evidence to suggest needed reform. He challenges parents, educators and citizens to see the connection between youth development and what he describes as a 'vast sociological experiment' that may forever change human relationships.

The '*Lightweb*' is known to all who use the Internet as a daily part of life. We easily connect to anyone around the world, not just via e-mail, but through a variety of on-line platforms and texting applications even on the smallest personal computing devices; we have access to a global storehouse of information; powerful search engines find documents, arguments and historical precedents, and almost any on-line question finds answers; we connect by audio and video with anyone, for free; we can build an on-line music and entertainment library without leaving home; we have palm-sized devices with dazzling capabilities for learning, recording, sharing and connecting.

The '*Darkweb*' is there too. Imposters, predators and porn sites lurk in the shadows on the Information Superhighway and all too easily lure unsuspecting users. Identity theft is an issue, as is the loss of privacy due to the 'data mining' practices of social media companies. On-line platforms allow stalkers to find the addresses and phone numbers of unwary users who are bullied, shamed and harassed mercilessly.

The hundreds of millions of young users who were never intended to be on social media (SM) are most vulnerable to security breaches, sometimes with lethal consequences.

Net evangelists cheer the virtual world with little reservation. Yet while there's scant evidence that daily on-line engagement contributes to, say, character development in our young, we do have evidence of Net dependence and SM addiction, with negative impacts on personal wellbeing and productivity.

The SM crisis is hard to miss: If kids (*the unintended users for whom the Net was not designed*) aren't safe on social media, if they can't effectively avoid the worst of the Darkweb, we've got a social catastrophe - a growing challenge to physical and mental health. The opportunity, simply put, is this: If social media is reformed with systemic safety features, if parents and teachers put sensible limits on screen time and age restrictions on Net use, we just might make the best of a very tough situation: benefit from the Lightweb by minimising its shadow.

'D is for Digital Danger' by David Penberthy – Sunday June 21st, 2015 couriermail.com .au'
Used with permission.

I don't think I have ever met a parent with kids on the cusp of their teenage years who doesn't worry about the excesses of the digital age. It's one of the few things that genuinely concerns me as a parent.

The enthusiasm with which so many young people, girls, will surrender their privacy by living every element of their lives in cyberspace. The extent to which so many young people, boys most troublingly, can and do access the most confronting brands of pornography at a time when their dealings with the opposite sex are very much a work in progress.

This week there were two court cases that brought these issues into sharp relief. The cases raised serious concerns about the way girls and boys learn to behave on-line.

They also raised troubling questions about whether sentencing guidelines enable the courts to take strong action against on-line predators.

The first was a federal case where the AFP busted Trevor Phillip Harris, 27, for soliciting dozens of lewd images from girls aged thirteen to seventeen and blackmailing them to provide him with more by threatening to upload the existing images for general view on-line.

The level of harassment was off the scale, with one of the young girls being contacted by this creep via Skype 133 times with his threats.

The second was a state matter involving a twenty-two-year-old Daniel Paul Guillard, who had uploaded and traded almost 300 images of the worst category of child pornography that's known as category five.

I'll spare you the details as outlined by the judge as to what category five involves. It will make you throw up.

The unfathomable feature of both these cases was that the judges in their sentencing remarks could not have been more scathing about the offenders, both of whom were as guilty as sin, but proceeded to hand them sentences which seem a million miles from community standards.

Harris was described as bereft of remorse or contrition. Gillard was told, rightly, that it was people like him who helped create a child-porn industry. Harris faced a maximum sentence of 10 years. He received a suspended sentence of two years and two months, being spared a single second's jail-time because he suffers from agoraphobia, a fear of public places, a condition which the judge said made his imprisonment problematic. He was required to pay a good behaviour bond of just $200.

Mention was made of the fact the Gillard had been suffering depression because of being dumped by his US-based fourteen-year-old girlfriend whom he met on-line.

I don't pretend to understand everything about sentencing principles but, to me, that doesn't sound like a mitigating circumstance. A twenty-two-year-old going out with a fourteen-year-old sounds like more evidence that the bloke is a weirdo.

But what about the utterly painless nature of the bonds these two were required to pay?

I got a parking fine in the city the other day for $58. That's close to what the court ordered Gillard to pay. A mate of mine ran a red turn-left arrow, driving at the crack of dawn, with no traffic to his right. He shouldn't have done it, obviously. His fine was $960. Almost ten times the bond imposed on Gillard and five times that suffered by Harris.

I'm all in favour of obeying the road rules, but it seems kind of sick that the only part of the criminal justice system which operates on a zero-tolerance basis involves lower-end traffic infringements.

There is, however, plenty of wiggle room for card-carrying perverts such as Harris and Gillard. The next time you're doing 69km/h in a 60km/h zone, maybe you could go to court explaining that you've got depression because your underage girlfriend ditched you, or that you were coming down with a bout of agoraphobia and put your foot to the floor.

You must feel for the police in these two cases. They bust their guts bringing these guys to justice, make their cases well and watch guilty men get flogged with a limp piece of lettuce.

The issue goes beyond the courts, though. One of the best columns I have read this year was by Nikki Gemmell in *The Australian,* which took aim at the hyper-sexualisation of young people in the digital age.

The column spoke about how so many girls were prepared to sacrifice their dignity and privacy because they simply believed it was now the norm to interact with boys in the form of a topless selfie, or worse.

At the other end of the spectrum, Gemmell wrote about how so many members of this generation of teenage boys risked growing up incapable of arousal by conventional sex or the naked female form, exposed as they were to 'sex' in its most aberrant and humiliating forms.

There is much of what Gemmell canvassed in the two cases explored here.

The Harris case demonstrates how teenage girls have both technology and the preparedness, even under duress, to take part in acts which less than a decade ago were beyond the realm of contemplation.

And, as for Gillard, without proffering it as an excuse, he is the sad, screwed-up product of a digital age where humans have been so degraded as to be dehumanised.

Stiffer jail sentences urged

A male nurse, Phillip Rohan Marcus Dibbs will be allowed to reapply to work as a health practitioner in ten years' time even though he is serving a jail sentence for multiple sex offences against a child. He was sentenced to six years in jail in December 2012 after pleading guilty to 13 child sex offences.

District Court Judge Stuart Durward described Dibb's conduct as 'depraved and disgusting.'

Dibbs surrendered his registration in 2012 and last year the Nursing and Midwifery Board brought disciplinary proceedings against him. Queensland Civil and Administrative Tribunal deputy president Judge Alexander. He ordered that Dibbs be disqualified from applying for registration for ten years from June 2015.

Why are we letting this man near children again? Don't we ever learn?

Resources for Parents and Kids

www.notforkids.info is a book for younger children to teach them how to respond if they see images online that make them feel uncomfortable.

www.itstimewetalked.com.au has fact sheets about how to start a conversation about pornography and the damage it can do.

Safety Tips for using Social Media

Parents/teachers/schools need to give children basic information on smartphone and social media usage such as how to protect their password, ensure personal safety on-line, the dangers of sexting, what constitutes cyber-bullying and when sharing nude images can become a criminal offence. They need to point out that porn does not reflect a healthy relationship and is a distorted view of sex; is not a template for how they should conduct their own intimate lives; and can forever spoil their enjoyment of having a normal sexual relationship with their partner. Some males who have viewed pornography for years, find that they become impotent when trying to have normal sexual relations with a woman.

Explain about kids being driven to suicide by cyber-bullying; those who now have a criminal record for sharing pornographic images and those hospitalised because they were on their phones when crossing the road.

Tell them what to do if they find themselves in a chatroom; how to respond if someone asks for a nude picture and how to end an uncomfortable text or e-mail conversation.

No matter how they're using them, here are a few things to keep in mind when they're being social on-line.

Don't use their real name:

It may seem obvious, but for many teens, it's not: Use an alias (a made-up name) for on sites such as MySpace. It's fine to tell trusted friends from school how to find their profile and what name you use for chatting and instant messaging, but keep their last name, age and other identifying information off their page if possible. It keeps a lot of shady characters from looking up other information about them, such as their address or what school they attend.

Be private:

Especially if they can't use an alias, they need to be extremely careful about who they let into their inner circle of friends on social networking sites. Consider setting their profile to private so they can carefully screen who can view their page.

Also, make sure they don't post photos that might give people the wrong idea about them. Here's a good rule of thumb: *If they'd be embarrassed for their favourite teacher or their best friend's parents to see it - it probably doesn't belong on their page.*

Keep their address and phone number to themselves:

Even if they screen their on-line friends carefully, it's good common sense to keep as much contact information to themselves as possible. They shouldn't share the name of their school or even their favourite after-school hangout on their page - even in a bulletin or invitation.

If they must list some contact information, list their secondary e-mail account, not the one they use for everyday stuff. Spammers and phishers love to grab e-mail addresses from Facebook and MySpace pages, so they should use an e-mail address with a good spam filter, too.

Set time limits:

Taking quizzes, writing comments and posting videos on their site or their friends' sites is a lot of fun, but it can easily eat up an entire afternoon. They need to set aside a specific amount of time - say, forty-five minutes to check their messages, send a few shout-outs and maybe play a quick game of Scrabulous.

If they're craving a chat, they need to ***make sure their homework is done*** and that they don't have family obligations before they hop on-line. Better yet, why not call their friend on the telephone or meet up with them to listen to music or watch their favourite TV show?

Be respectful:

Use the same sense of decency and etiquette that they would at school: i.e. they don't flirt with their friends' girlfriends and boyfriends; and apologise if they've hurt someone's feelings and avoid teasing, bullying or picking on others. The Internet has a karma all its own: What they dish out is going to make its way back to them; it's just a matter of time. (The same goes for kindness and good behaviour, of course.)

Your child isn't a little kid any more, and that means that by now, s/he should have mastered certain independence skills. Teens can do a lot and learning how to master certain everyday skills will motivate your child to learn more and feel like a big kid.

Chapter 2
Paedophiles

What is a paedophile?

A paedophile is a person who has a sustained sexual orientation toward children, generally aged 13 or younger. In most cases, the paedophile is at least sixteen years of age and at least five years older than the child. We know that paedophiles are overwhelmingly male, that their desire can fluctuate and that there can be some effectiveness in anti-libidinal medication to curb or reduce their sexual reactions, although researchers still hotly contest its efficiency.

Paedophilia is defined as a paraphilia which includes recurrent, intense sexually arousing fantasies, sexual urges or behaviours that involve children, non-human subjects, other non-consenting adults or the suffering or humiliation of oneself or one's partner.

Some paedophiles refrain from sexually approaching any child for their entire lives. At one end of the spectrum are those who prefer having sex with children – paedophiles – while at the other are people who will have sex with children because of the situation they find themselves in. It could be just out of curiosity; it could be because they don't feel as if children are going to judge them like adults will; it could be that they'll have sex with anything and children are just one of the spectrum; it could be a revenge-type scenario – he's in a relationship with somebody but feels disaffected in some way; doesn't have any power or control or feels as if his partner is dominating him – so he chooses children.

There are some who demonstrate a life-long fixation; it's their primary sexual focus. There are others who are periodically attracted to children, but not all the time. Some paedophiles will be repulsed and seek to avoid it, and others will give way to it because sexuality is a powerful driver of human behaviour.

Paedophilia can be characterised as either exclusive or non-exclusive. Exclusive paedophiles are attracted only to children. They show no interest in sexual partners who are not pre-pubescent children. Non-exclusive paedophiles are attracted to both adults and children. A large percentage of male paedophiles are homosexual or bisexual in orientation to children, meaning they are attracted to male and female adults and/or both male and female children.

They place themselves in positions where they can easily meet children. The internet has become a common hunting ground to prey on children. Today more and more kids are using Facebook accounts. By creating a profile displaying one's personal information these children are indirectly helping paedophiles find their next target. They can befriend children and manipulate, trap and lure their targets into a false sense of trust.

Some paedophiles may ***pretend they're someone else***, such as a classmate. Others develop friendship with children and then arrange times and places, so they can act upon and fulfil their sexual desires.

Most people imagine paedophiles as ugly old men dressed in trench coats, hiding in the bushes, waiting to snatch young children off the street. However, recent television shows have exposed paedophiles as local neighbours, trusted friends, clergy, babysitters, teachers and even family members.

Many people assume that only males are paedophiles, however female paedophiles do exist. These female predators display similar behaviour such as irrational thoughts, repetitive thoughts and many suffer from psychiatric disorders or substance abuse problems. Also, there's a higher likelihood that they've been sexually abused as a child. As children, they lacked the ability to control the situation. By sexually assaulting children, paedophiles attempt to re-live the trauma they experienced and learn how to master it. A complete role-reversal that in their minds gives them the upper hand and prevents them from being targeted again.

The Catholic Church frowns upon certain sexual behaviour with children. A great deal of hypocrisy surrounds the sex abuse scandal in the Catholic Church. In many cases, the clergy were paedophiles. These priests sexually abused minors, primarily male altar servers and exerted power over these boys. Yet Catholic children remain vulnerable to sexual offenders regardless of their public façade.

The children who fell victim to the clergy were easily accessible, vulnerable and unthreatening. These priests who engaged in sexual behaviour with youth should be held responsible for their actions. The Church should take the proper steps to correct this type of behaviour and have their paedophilic priests seek treatment for their disorder and be kept away from children.

There are patterns to paedophiles' manipulations; consistent techniques by which they groom the trust of the child and those around them. Often the child knows the abuser and the man can offend through the position of trust. So, a parent or step parent could be the abuser. It could be a mentor or sports coach or often through friendship or association with the family. ***The child is encouraged to keep secrets*** and the paedophile tries to isolate them from other people. Some may offer bribes.

Abusers find areas of common interest with the child; they flatter their intelligence and insight, give them gifts and pay attention to them more than their parents do. They conspire to create situations where they and the child will be together. Isolation is important to the paedophile – not only does it lessen the chance of detection but forms a false but flattering sense of conspiracy with the target.

There's no type of child who is more vulnerable than another; targets come from all sections of society and different types of families – not just broken homes as is commonly thought.

What causes Paedophilia?

Biological and environmental factors contribute to paedophilia. The abusers have problems with self-control; have extreme urges and cognitive distortions. Many experts believe that disorders for sexual preferences emerge from childhood experiences.

Can Paedophilia be treated?

Although most experts don't think a person's feelings of paedophilia are curable, therapy may help them manage those feelings and not act on them. Some patients at high risk of committing sexual offenses may need medications to reduce their sex drive.

Not only do television shows expose paedophiles, but there are new sexual offender disclosure laws, websites that track convicted sexual offenders and more investigations of paedophilia, especially after the sex abuse scandal in the Catholic Church. The sexual urges associated with paedophilia may never permanently disappear. Most treatment primarily focuses on preventing further offenses, rather than changing sexual orientation.

Research does show that the greatest percentage of people who commit these offences have been offended against themselves. When they're apprehended, some child pornography users express relief because they did not believe they would be able to stop offending by themselves. Others express no remorse at all – have no feelings of guilt for their actions.

For psychological treatment to be beneficial, three things need to occur: the patient is motivated to change; the therapist develops a rapport with the paedophile; and sometimes external inducements or coercion to take treatment, such as revoking parole, is exercised.

Are Paedophiles only attracted to children?

Some paedophiles may be as attracted to adults as they are to children, but it's hard to know how common that is. That's because most paedophilia research is based on people who were arrested for sexual offenses against children and they may tend to exaggerate their sexual interest in adults to seem more normal.

One Paedophile's Story

One man was shocked when he admitted to himself that he was a paedophile. He realised that he had always known that he was attracted to boys, but somehow, he'd avoided labelling himself. After all, he was married, attracted to women and had never done anything with a child. The force of the label was like a nuclear bomb going off inside his head. The word was so ugly, and he felt evil and dirty.

His wife was away, and he didn't sleep for three nights and thought seriously of killing himself. He was not a religious man, but he prayed that those feelings would be taken from him. What he realised after he admitted he was a paedophile was that there weren't many associations set up to help paedophiles from acting on their urges, so he set one up in Australia entitled Virtuous Pedophiles. It permits membership only to those who denounce child abuse and actively avoid temptation.

Paedophiles/Child Molesters

The term paedophile is often used erroneously to describe child sexual abusers or molesters. To achieve sexual gratification through the abuse of a child, you must be able to suspend ideas of wrongfulness; must be able to over-ride concerns for the welfare of the child to meet your needs. That normally requires the absence of empathic feelings.

Not all paedophiles are child molesters (or vice versa). Child molesters are defined by their acts; pedophiles are defined by their desires.

Understanding what makes child molesters tick, as opposed to paedophiles, is more complex. Ninety-nine percent of offenders in this category will initially refuse to discuss why they've committed the offences. Some sex offenders have no idea why they've done it because they really don't want to seriously look at their aberrant behaviour. They don't want to admit to other adults that they have a large porn collection or about their sexual fantasies. However, if they don't want to re-offend, they need to seriously look at those behaviours and do something about it. If not, then the chances of them being able to hold back from re-offending are slim.

Hunting predators

Taskforce Argos officer Paul Griffiths hunts internet paedophiles and has been nominated for a Pride of Australia Heroism Medal. Since joining Argos in 2009, Mr Griffiths and his team have helped identify more than 300 targets of internet paedophiles.

He and his colleagues are still rescuing hundreds of child targets and sparing thousands more from unspeakable abuse.

He brought down a global on-line paedophile network when he identified Shannon Grant McCoole, a South Australian carer as being a paedophile. Shannon was the administrator of the 45,000-member internet site that showed hundreds of thousands of hard-core child abuse videos and images.

Mr McCoole was a Families Southern Australia carer with access to children. Mr. Griffiths analysed the administrator's language, peculiar greetings and usernames and found similar instances on unrelated internet forums.

After Shannon was arrested, detectives assumed his on-line identity and reeled in associates, then shut down the site. Mr McCoole pleaded guilty to eighteen child sex-related offences.

Since that arrest the investigators have tracked down more than one hundred offenders and rescued sixty-five children from abuse.

Pornography

The downloading of child pornography is out of control with videos and still images becoming more extreme and showing increasingly younger children. The proliferation of smartphones and tablets has made it more difficult for parents to keep tabs on who their children are communicating with. Gone are the days when police could effectively advise parents to keep the home computer in a communal area, because the children have them with them at school and at friends' homes.

In July 2015, Children's Commissioner Megan Mitchell has called for a review into whether Australian kids are being adequately protected from exposure to hardcore and violent pornography on-line. 'Children's ready access and exposure to violent and pornographic imagery through on-line platforms poses real risks of distorting their attitudes to sex and relationships,' she said.

'I strongly support a review of how well regulatory and other measures are working to reduce the negative impact of pornography.'

She added that children needed better education, at home and school, about sex and healthy relationships, but other options such as opt-in porn filters need to be part of the solution.

Some governments are trying to block explicit pornography at a network level.

The dangers of pornography

Watching pornography at a very young age can result in a completely warped idea of what normal bodies look like and how normal bodies react when another person 'turns them on.' Those who are addicted to pornography are completely unaware of what intimacy means and only see others as sexual objects. The idea of romance is foreign to them.

Many teens compare themselves to how the 'stud's' anatomy is so much sexier than theirs. They look down at themselves and realise that they fall short in the penis department. They look at their normal chests and biceps and compare them against the studs 'performing' in the pornography and again believe they fall short.

Females, young and old, shown in pornography look nothing like the average woman or girl, so the boys find they can't become sexually stimulated by normal-looking females, so revert to masturbating while watching pornography or pay a prostitute for their services.

These males can't relate to females without wondering what she would look and act like if she was naked in bed. They have vivid pictures of this in their minds – and the girls often intuit this desire so become embarrassed and feel as if they've been mentally undressed.

Young boys who, through curiosity, put the word 'porn' into a Google search usually expect to see a couple having sex or simply show beautiful naked female bodies. Instead, they see savage sex performed on females; brutal acts that leave the woman battered and bruised. They see anal sex on young girls and boys.

The average Australian boy is eleven when he has his first exposure to pornography. Many innocently click onto what is known as 'gonzo porn' that shows anal sex, lesbians having sex and even gangbangs. Some are repelled by the visions, but others get 'hooked.'

The degradation of women, with violence and humiliation are shown in most of these sites. Many experts believe that porn has become a health emergency, not only for the teens and pre-teens exposed to it, but by the men who have grown up watching it find that normal sex does nothing for them.

This kind of hard porn is no longer hidden but has become main-stream and it's now difficult for people to even find soft core porn.

Young teenage girls have their virginity taken from them by boys who have watched porn and think they must mimic what they've observed on the porn sites. These young girls are often left with serious sexual injuries with vaginal and anal tearing.

The boys think this is how a relationship with a girl works and is mortified when her mother and father come to his home to explain to his parents the damage he has done to their daughter. The boy's shocked parents are often unaware that their son has been indulging in pornography (sometimes for years without their knowledge) let alone that he used violent sex on his fragile young virgin girlfriend.

As they mature these teens need higher and higher levels of violence to appease their appetite for watching sex that's all about punishment, domination and vengeance and there's nothing loving in the acts they're driven to perform. As grown men, they find it impossible to get or sustain an erection when they must indulge in non-violent sex.

Parents play an important role in preventing kids from accessing hard-core porn. They need to have a discussion with their sons when they reach ten to explain the differences between normal sex and the kind of sex that is shown on pornography sites. Instead of pornography being the only sexual education received by vulnerable pre-pubescent children, we must start to fill the void, so pornography does not become the sex education of our youth.

Parents are encouraged to install filters and software to block explicit adult sites. Unfortunately, as earlier mentioned, this does not protect their child from entering chat rooms – where there are no filters.

While there is no doubt that the internet has made offending easier for those who would have offended anyway, it's also clear that it has increased the likelihood of people graduating from viewing child pornography to abusing children. Research is showing that pornography is by far the biggest indicator of what a person's actual preference is and that if they have lots of porn, it's not going to help them stop re-offending. Someone who's viewing a lot of child porn is going to be more at risk of committing offences against children. The more they see of anything, the more acceptable it's going to become – no matter what it is.

Some offenders start off viewing 'legal' porn, go to more bizarre things, moved on to bestiality, then children, and then move on to contacting children and offend. If he started with pornography at around twelve or thirteen, then by the time he's twenty-one or twenty-two he's trying to get kids through the internet.

In older paedophiles, the behaviour is ingrained; they've convinced themselves that they're not actually doing anything wrong. Then they meet with other like-minded men (usually on the internet) who share pornography which reinforces their idea that they're not doing anything wrong.

Gang rape is one of the many unwanted offshoots of men's growing pornography consumption. Growing numbers of gang rape victims is attributed to young men's consumption of pornography that fuels unhealthy views of sex. One young man will engage with a young woman for sex and then others are invited in – usually without the permission of the woman.

On July 15, 2019 the UK will be the first country in the world to demand age verification for people viewing pornography online to verify that they are 18 or over. Porn sites that sell adult content or provide it free will have to employ companies to provide age checks.

Chapter 3
Bullying

Every child has the right to an education and has the right to be safe. Adults working the school systems have a duty to provide a safe school environment for all students. Safe schools are:

- Free from violence;
- Nurturing, caring and respectful of everyone;
- Physically and psychologically healthy;
- Advocates of sensible risk taking;
- Enhance the self-esteem of all.

What is bullying?

Bullying is a pattern of constant, daily fault-finding, criticism, segregation, exclusion and undermining that occurs for weeks or months. Each incident can be trivial, and on their own do not represent an offence or grounds for disciplinary action. Bullying occurs on average every seven minutes and the episode is brief, approximately 37 seconds long. However, emotional scars from bullying can last a lifetime.

Recovery from a bullying experience can take between two to five years, and some people never fully recover. Bullying differs from harassment and assault because the latter can result from a single incident or a small number of incidents, whereas bullying tends to be an accumulation of many small incidents over a long period of time.

Sixty per cent of children identified as bullies before they're eight years old, will have a criminal conviction by the age of twenty-four, so it's important that parents, teachers and the community do something to curb their bullying. If the bullies don't end up in jail, they'll end up involved in other violent behaviour like workplace bullying or spousal abuse.

Those who carry their bullying behaviour with them into adulthood often develop a roster of problems: alcoholism, anti-social personality disorders and mental health disorders. If his or her behaviour is not treated, the bully can grow up to bully his/her spouse, children and co-workers. Bullying becomes a habit, an easy method for the bully to get what s/he wants.

The children who manage to ward off the bully tend to have better social and conflict management skills. So, this is where parents and teachers should place their emphasis in teaching the bullying children to use better interpersonal skills. Those children who don't bully are better able to assert themselves without becoming aggressive or confrontational. Instead, they work out compromises and devise alternative solutions. These children appear to be more aware of people's feelings (empathetic skills) and are the children who can be most helpful in resolving disputes and assisting other children to get help.

Targets of Bullies

Children who have been repeatedly targeted by a bully show certain behaviours and attitudes. Sometimes these behaviours are inconsistent with the child's typical behaviour. Many children are too embarrassed and humiliated to report being targeted and worry that speaking out will lead to even more abuse.

Most children joke around with each other, call each other games or rough-house - and yet these incidents are not normally called bullying. The difference lies in the relationship of the bully and the target and the intent of that interaction. It normally occurs between individuals who are *not* friends and there's a perceived power difference between the bully and the target. The bully is usually bigger, tougher, physically stronger, or can intimidate others.

Bullies and their targets come from all levels of socio-economic situations. Essentially, they're looking for power that they're not getting or feeling anywhere else. Bullying is gender-neutral and can range from gang attacks to playground bullying.

Researchers still can't explain why young girls act out their aggression in different ways from boys, but their biology is believed to be the main factor. Girls use whispering campaigns and psychological bullying that their teachers find hard to detect. With girls, it mainly comes in the form of gossiping, spreading lies, backbiting, ruining reputations, or social isolation that excludes one or more children from their group.

Girls may be biologically hot-wired to engage in sophisticated, non-violent forms of aggression that can hurt just as much as a punch in the jaw from a boy. It's now believed that the non-physical conflict or indirect aggression could be as dangerous to children as physical bullying.

Girls often swap social media passwords to show loyalty amongst friends, but this can be used against a girl ousted from a group. Even though the girl might change her password, often her enemies have changed it first leaving her vulnerable to hate campaigns that can push kids as young as ten to contemplate suicide.

When caught, many girls use tactics such as apologising or crying - that gets them out of trouble but doesn't solve the underlying problem causing their bullying. Their targets feel that the bullying was directed towards excluding them from their peer group.

Girls have different responses to authority than boys and in the way, they deal with problems. If they're bullied, they're more likely to skip school when problems arise. Many use truancies to deal with their bullies, and often their teachers and parents miss the real reason for their truancy. All truancy should be investigated to find the reasons behind the absence from school.

Boys tend to defend themselves and answer back but can get themselves into worse trouble. Bullying amongst boys is usually physical and involves hitting, shoving and sometimes weapons.

For the child growing up in a dysfunctional or abusive home environment, bullying becomes a compulsive and obsessive behaviour. The bully must have a target, so s/he can displace his or her own aggression. The bullying child's parents may lack parental skills because they too were brought up by parents who lacked appropriate behaviour skills; and their parents were likely brought up in that same abusive climate.

The cycle must be broken. This is where schools can play a major role - *but only if they enforce anti-bullying policies and support and help both the bullied child and the bully*.

Children who pick on other children could come from dysfunctional homes or homes with a lack of adult supervision. They could be targets of violence themselves, learning that violence is an acceptable way to interact with others, or they could have missed a stage in their development and experienced a delay in their emotional development. Bullies may have parents who ignore them or have mothers who abused alcohol or drugs while they were pregnant. Violent television programs also reinforce that it's okay to act aggressively.

Ultimately though, bullying is behaviour and behaviour is a choice. Therefore, bullying is a choice. It's the bully's choice to bully. A bad choice – but a choice!

While a poor home environment, poor parenting, poor role models may influence the bully - they are not a cause. Many children have poor home environments but do not choose to bully; therefore, these factors cannot be used as a specific excuse for bullying.

The memory of individual school yard bullying remains clear and unblemished for many adults long after they leave school. Any child or adult can tell you about a time s/he was bullied, or s/he saw someone s/he knew being bullied. Bullies seek power. Bullying can be multiple episodes or consist of one single interaction. The intention of the bully is to put the target in distress in some way.

The most despicable bullies on this earth are terrorists, murderers, rapists, paedophiles and pimps. These dregs of the earth all have one insatiable and obsessive need - to control others. They know of no other way to live life except to overpower others. However, they're cowards and have yellow streaks down their backbones. Anyone who feels confident about him- or herself does not need to use power to influence or control others.

This control is gained through terror, intimidation, harassment or just plain aggressiveness. Extroverted bullies tend to be shouters and screamers - are highly visible and bully from the top. A discussion becomes a debate and often ends up in a shouting match. They manipulate others into believing that *they* caused the bullying behaviour.

Introverted bullies (the most dangerous types) tend to sit in the background and recruit others to do the bullying for them.

Bullies are cunning, conniving, scheming, calculating, sadistic, violent, cruel, nasty, ruthless, treacherous, pre-meditated, exploitive, parasitic, obnoxious, opportunist, ominous, menacing, sinister, ferocious, forceful, annoying, and aggressive. They are experts in the use of sarcasm but lack communication, interpersonal and social skills. Some rely excessively or exclusively on phones, texting, emails or third parties and other strategies for avoiding face-to-face contact.

Bullies lack emotional intelligence. Emotional intelligence helps people understand and control their own emotions. It also helps them recognise and respond correctly to others' emotions. Those with emotional intelligence recognise emotions in others and know how to control their reactions to those emotions. They also know their own emotions and how to control them when they're getting upset or angry. Bullies are either born without emotional intelligence, or they suppress it by copying their defective role models. Often extensive counselling is the only way to change their destructive behaviour.

Bullying tends to peak in sixth grade and diminish slightly every year thereafter. Most teens will encounter bullying at some point in middle school. The best way to protect your child is to sit down and discuss behaviours common in middle school such as relational aggression. Teens who are being bullied may try to hide the fact from family members or teachers, so be sure you know the signs of bullying to take quick action.

The teen years offer up several challenges, including puberty, middle school, and the possibility that at some point in the next few years your child may encounter bullying.

Bullies seem to turn up everywhere and bullying is on the rise, fuelled by technology and often-times by a culture that permits or ignores it altogether.

In fact, forty-eight percent of children (almost half of all children) say they've been the target of bullying at one time or another.

Bullying during the middle school years is especially common as children attempt to establish their place and their social status amongst others. Unfortunately, that may mean singling out another child, a behaviour sometimes referred to as relational aggression or mob bullying. Bullies can be clever, and their behaviour can go unnoticed for quite a while.

School Bullying

Schools are a prime location for bullying. Most of the school bullying occurs in or close to school buildings. Many bullies try to pass off acts of aggression as roughhousing. Most targets don't report the bullying. Occasionally, a target provokes the attack of their bully. These targets tease their bullies, making themselves a target by egging the bully on. These targets often don't know when to stop their provocation and usually aren't able to defend themselves when the balance of power shifts to the bully. Body language is everything when school bullies pick their prey.

Physical defects, like big ears, speech problems or a limp, don't normally play a role, but body language and level of self-esteem have everything to do with whether the child will or will not be bullied. Targets are encouraged to stand tall, say, *'No'* in a loud voice and make eye contact. If targets are taught how to react, they can curb the problem. A bully needs an audience, so if witnesses simply leave the area when a situation happens, **and they report the bullying** - the bullies lose their audience and must account for their unacceptable behaviour.

Only twenty-five per cent of students report that teachers intervene in bullying situations, while seventy-one per cent of teachers believe they always intervene.

Past research showed that back in 1996 most students (60 per cent) were never directly involved in any kind of bullying, as targets or as bullies (Psychology Today, September 1996). Since then, most students have witnessed bullying incidents at the schoolyard. The unfortunate thing is they do nothing to stop the bullying.

Why don't other students help the target?

They're reluctant to report bullying because they fear retaliation from the bully themselves. Children who are not bullies or targets have a powerful role to play in shaping the behaviour of other children. It's the 52 per cent of children within a school who are not bullied or targeted who hold the key to stop bullying. Children need to be encouraged to speak up on behalf of children they see being bullied. Students who witness bullying have the potential to reduce bullying by refusing to watch bullying, reporting bullying incidents and/or distracting the bully. The key to a successful anti-bullying campaign is to involve everyone in working toward a solution.

The bullying cycle works on witnesses as follows:

- They fear that teachers will confront the bully in such a way that the witnesses are now at risk.
- They fear that their confidentiality will be breached and/or their status within their peer group will be compromised.

Bullies survive by creating the myth that if their behaviour is reported, they will retaliate swiftly and severely. This threat paralyses the targets and witnesses into a code of silence that allows the bully to extend his/her reign of terror.

Unfortunately, many teachers and school staff don't know how to intervene properly, so the bullying continues. This leads to more helplessness for the targets and gives more power to the bullies who know they will get away with their bullying, and/or feel the school has condoned their behaviour.

Teachers need to make it safe for their students to report any bullying incident. They accomplish this by respecting the anonymity of the target and witnesses. Until the targets and witnesses trust that this will happen - bullying will go unreported, and bullies will be encouraged to continue their actions. Bullies must know the consequences for bullying and *schools must consistently enforce the rules*. Bullies need counselling, so they can learn how to behave in a socially acceptable manner, as their targets need to learn assertiveness and have confidence that any reported bullying will be dealt with swiftly and effectively by authority figures.

Bullies are often socially accepted until their mid-teens. Despite their aggressive behaviour, they can even enjoy social popularity with their peers. But, by late adolescence, the bully's popularity begins to fade. Bullies lose their popularity as they get older and are eventually disliked by most students. The paths of the mid-teen bully and his or her former target rarely cross. By that age, teens have clearly defined their social set. Tragically, the bullies find themselves becoming more excluded by their peers and often seek out alliances with gangs of other isolated individuals. These teen gangs often get into serious trouble with the law.

By senior high school, most regular bullying incidents are a thing of the past, but the memories of their abuse haunts targets and they continue to avoid their bully. Some carry their emotional scars for a lifetime.

Ignoring the bullying

'Kids will be kids' or 'boys will be boys' were often the response by adults when a child complains about bullying. But we now know that bullying is assault, and targets are protected by law when that happens. Bullies learn young that words can be used to hurt - so they experiment. They want to experience the feeling of power that comes with being able to manipulate someone. For some kids, it's something they try once. In others it becomes a way of life and every situation becomes a power struggle - with their parents, their teachers, their siblings and their playmates.

The bully does not have to be the nicest, best-looking or the funniest kid. S/he just must know how to form a group and then take charge. They make the rules and decide whether they will play with a new kid or make his/her life miserable via bullying.

One daughter was caught shoplifting. The family was horrified but were even more upset months later when the full story was revealed. The girl was stealing to avoid being attacked by a bully. She was ordered to steal, told what to steal, and if she didn't bring the goods to school - she was in for it. The fact that the bully had so much control over the girl that she would take the chance of being arrested to avoid a bully, should tell us the power these bullies have over others.

Signs of Bullying

There are ways to detect bullies and determine whether your child has had to face them. If you suspect your teen has had a run in with a bully at school, on the bus, in the cafeteria, or even on the ball field, there will be clues in her behaviour and appearance, such as:

- Withdrawing from their favourite activities;
- Anxiety about travelling to and from school;
- Requesting parents to drive or collect them;
- Changing route of travel;
- Avoiding regular times for travelling to and from school;
- Unwillingness to go to school;

- Declining interest in school or after school activities;
- Deterioration in educational performance;
- Pattern of physical illnesses (e.g. headaches, stomach aches);
- Withdrawing from their friends or social circle;
- Wanting to run away;
- Loss of concentration;
- Anger (may or may not be directed at you);
- Stress;
- Crying, depression, sudden rages;
- Volatile emotions;
- Consistently missing the bus;
- Comes home from school overly hungry;
- Has trouble sleeping;
- Unexplained changes either in mood or behaviour (it may be particularly noticeable before returning to school after weekends or more specifically after longer school holidays);
- Torn clothes, backpack, or other personal items;
- Missing or damaged school items, such as books, homework, lunch box, or band instrument;
- Wanting to take protection to school such as a knife or a gun;
- Bruises and/or scrapes; has been in physical fights;
- Loss of or increase in appetite;
- Visible signs of anxiety or distress – stammering, withdrawing, nightmares, difficulty in sleeping, crying, not eating, vomiting, bedwetting;
- Spontaneous out-of-character comments about either pupils or teachers;
- Increased requests for money or stealing money;
- Reluctance and/or refusal to say what's troubling them;

- 'Loses' things – a sign that someone is stealing the child's items.

Those signs do not necessarily mean that a pupil is being bullied. If repeated or occurring in combination, those signs do warrant investigation to establish what is affecting the pupil.

If the signals are there, it's time for a talk with your teen. Many teens will be reluctant and embarrassed to share details of the bullying, and some may even feel they deserve to be bullied. Others will worry that the bullies will increase their torment if you or they tell on them.

Sit down and ask if there have been any problems or bullying issues at school, or if they've encountered someone who is trying to make their lives difficult. If the answer is yes, offer up suggestions on how they may handle the bully in question. Sometimes, a simple response such as, 'Don't talk to me that way!' or 'Stop annoying me!' may be enough to deter the bullies or quiet them down.

Role play situations your teen might encounter with possible solutions to stop the abuse. Encourage your teen to keep away from the bully, and to stick with one or two friends when the bully is present.

It's also important that your child understand that it's not his/her fault that s/he's being bullied. Be sure s/he knows that s/he can ask teachers or the bus driver for help, if the behaviour continues, and help him/her find ways to inform adults about bullying, without sounding like s/he's tattling on a child.

If your child's attempts to end the bullying fail to work, and the bullying continues, it's time to call the school and ask for a meeting with the principal and/or the teacher. Be very clear that you expect the behaviour to end, and that you expect a follow up by the school in several weeks to make sure it hasn't returned. As a last resort, ask to meet with the other child's parents, but do so only with the teacher, guidance counsellor or principal present.

Bullies use different kinds of bullying:

Physical Bullies:

They act out their anger in physical ways. They resort to hitting or kicking their targets or damaging the target's property. Of all the types of bullies, this one is easiest to identify because his/her behaviour is so obvious. This is the type of bully our imagination conjures up when we picture a bully. As they get older, physical bullies can become more aggressive in their attacks. As adults this aggressive attitude is so deeply ingrained in the bully's personality that serious long-term counselling is required to change the behaviour.

Verbal Bullies:

It's quite difficult for a target to ignore this type of bully. They use words to hurt and humiliate, resorting to name-calling, insulting, teasing and making racist, chauvinistic or paternalistic comments. While this type of bullying does not result in physical scars, its effects can be devastating. It's often the easiest form of attack for a bully. It's quick and painless for the bully, but often remarkably harmful for the target.

Pornography:

Pornography has been a traditional outlet for sexual frustration, and probably always will be. Its acceptability is determined by current social values. Most young boys secretly indulge occasionally to see what they're missing. The harder the pornographic content, the more abusive it tends to be. The individual's need and hence dependency on pornography is directly proportional to that individual's feelings of sexual inadequacy.

Bullies who were targets:

Some bullies have been bullied or abused themselves. There is evidence that many murderers, especially those involving serial killings, have received brain damage from parental beatings. Those beatings can leave them with the inability to control their violent tendencies.

The first-time bullies get a taste of their own medicine, they run whining to authorities for protection. They bully to feel competent and to get some relief from their own feelings of powerlessness. They are stuck between the state of a being a target and a being a bully and are usually the most difficult to identify because they, at first glance, appear to be targets of other bullies. They are usually impulsive and react quickly to intentional or unintentional physical encounters, claiming self-defence for their actions. Rather than lashing out at his or her bully, this target needs to learn how to avoid other bullies.

Many abusers, molesters, harassers and bullies who end up in court because of their actions insist that they too were targets.

These bullies seem to rely on their past problems as a target to gain supporters. Such 'do-gooders' will take advantage of any form of support they can get to evade taking responsibility for their actions. When asked to account for the way they choose to behave, bullies use a variety of strategies to evade accountability such as denial, counter-attack and feigned victimhood.

They're experts at buck-passing. They have not learned how to take responsibility for their actions, lack self-discipline, and will often blame someone else for why they reacted as they did.

Female Bullies:

Society assumes that in a violent situation, there is a male aggressor and a female target, but females can be as vicious as males. Female bullies are spiteful, devious, manipulative and vengeful. These individuals use gossip and backstabbing to undermine, discredit or devaluate other's contributions. They have poorly-defined moral and ethical boundaries and put others down to make themselves feel important. They are experts in the use of sarcasm but lack communication, interpersonal and social skills.

Group Bullies/Exclusion Bullies:

These are predominantly female bullies who exclude their targets from feeling part of a group. They exploit the feeling of insecurity in their targets, by ambushing their targets and convincing peers to exclude or reject the target. They often use the same tricks that the verbal bullies use with their targets to isolate them. Spreading nasty rumours about the target is part of the pattern. It can be an extremely harmful form of bullying especially in children when they are making their first social connections, because it excludes the target from his/her peer group.

Those who are excluded

Targeted individuals relate to themselves and the world around them differently than non-targeted peers. In a study of temporary social exclusion, researchers found that excluded children felt that time was dragging by and thought that life was less meaningful than those who were not excluded. They were also less willing to reflect on themselves.

Being excluded may increase the risk of suicide

In part, because of the effects already mentioned, individuals who have been socially excluded may be at higher risk of suicide. Studies have shown that even temporary social exclusion can cause cognitive and emotional changes that match those seen before suicide attempts. For instance, socially excluded individuals tend to display little to no emotional expression, just like pre-suicidal individuals.

Exclusion Leads to Increased Aggression

Social exclusion can also lead to increased aggression from targets. This aggression may be physical, verbal or relational, or a combination of all three. In other words, the target quickly becomes the bully. This may be particularly notable in girls, who tend to socially exclude others when they believe they are about to be excluded.

Sexual Harassment

Very few records have been kept about the number of children who have been sexually harassed at school, but many are not only harassed by other students but by school staff as well. Sexual harassment in school is no different than sexual harassment elsewhere.

Schools need to include sexual harassment in their anti-bullying policies and post them where they're visible by all students. Students must understand that sexual comments (including those relating to sexual preference) are not permitted and are a form of bullying.

Students and witnesses to sexual harassment would deal with it the same way they would deal with bullying incidents.

One sexual harassment code states that sexual harassment can include one or more of the following unacceptable behaviours:

- Unwelcome sexual remarks such as jokes, innuendoes, teasing, and verbal abuse;

- Taunts about a person's body, attire, age, sexual preference, marital status;
- Displays of pornographic, offensive or derogatory pictures;
- Practical jokes that cause awkwardness or embarrassment;
- Unwelcome invitations or requests, whether indirect or explicit;
- Intimidation;
- Leering or suggestive gestures;
- Condescension or paternalistic treatment that undermines self-respect;
- Unnecessary physical contact such as touching, patting, pinching, punching or physical assault.

Students should also be aware that complaints can be made to their applicable Human Rights Commission or Equal Rights Commission if a school fails in their duty of care and does not stop the behaviour. One sexual harassment law states that:

'Any person responsible for any act of sexual harassment, any supervisor, manager, or person in a position of authority who is aware of the sexual harassment and does not take immediate and appropriate action, (as well as the company) will be named in any complaint brought before the Human Rights Commission.'

This means that teachers can no longer 'look the other way' and pretend that sexual harassment is not occurring. They must step in and stop the harassment; otherwise they too could be charged with sexual harassment because they condoned the behaviour.

Pupils who Bully

Physical Aggression: This behaviour is more common among boys than girls. It includes pushing, shoving, punching, kicking, poking and tripping people up. It may also take the form of severe physical assault. While boys commonly engage in 'mess fights,' they can often be used as a disguise for physical harassment or inflicting pain.

Damage to Property: Personal property can be the focus of attention for the bully: this may result in damage to clothing, school books and other learning material or interference with a pupil's locker or bicycle. The contents of school bags and pencil cases may be scattered on the floor. Items of personal property may be defaced, broken, stolen or hidden.

Extortion: Demands for money may be made, often accompanied by threats (sometimes carried out) in the event of the target not promptly 'paying up.' Targets' lunches, lunch vouchers or lunch money may be taken. Targets may also be forced into theft of property for delivery to the bully. Sometimes, this tactic is used with the sole purpose of incriminating the target.

Intimidation: Some bullying behaviour takes the form of intimidation; it is based on the use of very aggressive body language with the voice being used as a weapon. Particularly upsetting to targets can be the so-called 'look' - a facial expression that conveys aggression and/or dislike.

Abusive Telephone Calls or texts: The abusive anonymous telephone call or text is a form of verbal intimidation or bullying. The anonymous phone call is very prevalent where teachers are the targets of bullying.

Exclusion and Isolation: This form of bullying behaviour seems to be more prevalent among girls. A certain person is deliberately isolated, excluded or ignored by some or the entire class group. This practice is usually initiated by the person engaged in bullying behaviour. It may be accompanied by writing insulting remarks about the target on blackboards or in public places, by passing around notes about or drawings of the target or by whispering insults about them loud enough to be heard.

Name Calling: Persistent name-calling directed at the same individual(s), that hurts, insults or humiliates should be regarded as a form of bullying behaviour. Most name-calling of this type refers to physical appearance, e.g. 'big ears,' size or clothes worn.

Accent or distinctive voice characteristics may attract negative attention. Academic ability can also provoke name-calling. This tends to operate at two extremes; first, there are those who are singled out for attention because they're perceived to be slow, or weak, academically. These pupils are often referred to as 'dummies,' 'dopes' or 'donkeys.'

At the other extreme are those who, because they're perceived as high achievers, are labelled 'swots,' 'brain-boxes,' 'licks,' 'teachers' pets,' etc.

Teasing: This behaviour usually refers to the good-natured banter that goes on as part of the normal social interchange between mainly young people. However, when this teasing extends to very personal remarks aimed again and again at one individual about appearance, clothing, personal hygiene or involves references of an uncomplimentary nature to members of one's family, particularly if couched in sexual innuendo, then it assumes the form of bullying. Or it may take the form of suggestive remarks about a pupil's sexual orientation.

Bullying of School Personnel

Bullying of school personnel by means of physical assault, damage to property, verbal abuse, threats to people's families etc.

Teacher Bullying:

A teacher may, unwittingly or otherwise, engage in, instigate or reinforce bullying behaviour in several ways:

- Humiliating directly or indirectly, a pupil who is particularly academically weak or outstanding, or vulnerable in other ways;
- Using any gesture or expression of a threatening or intimidatory nature, or any form of degrading physical contact or exercise;
- Using sarcasm or other insulting or demanding form of language when addressing pupils;
- Making negative comments about a pupil's appearance or background.

Helping the Target

Here's a story about a boy who *did* step in to help another student:

'One day, when I was a freshman in high school, I saw a kid from my class walking home from school. His name was Kyle. It looked like he was carrying all his books. I thought to myself, 'Why would anyone bring home all his books on a Friday? He must really be a nerd.'

I had quite a weekend planned (parties and a football game with my friends tomorrow afternoon), so I shrugged my shoulders and went on.

As I was walking, I saw a bunch of kids running toward him. They ran at him, knocking all his books out of his arms and tripping him so he landed in the dirt. His glasses went flying, and I saw them land in the grass about ten feet from him. He looked up and I saw this terrible sadness in his eyes.

My heart went out to him. So, I jogged over to him and as he crawled around looking for his glasses, and I saw a tear in his eye. As I handed him his glasses, I said, 'Those guys are jerks. They really should get lives.'

He looked at me and said, 'Hey thanks!'

There was a big smile on his face. It was one of those smiles that showed real gratitude.

I helped him pick up his books and asked him where he lived. As it turned out, he lived near me, so I asked him why I had never seen him before. He said he had gone to private school before now.

I would have never hung out with a private school kid before. We talked all the way home, and I carried some of his books. He turned out to be a pretty cool kid. I asked him if he wanted to play a little football with my friends. He said yes. We hung out all weekend and the more I got to know Kyle, the more I liked him, and my friends thought the same of him.

Monday morning came, and there was Kyle with the huge stack of books again. I stopped him and said, 'Boy, you are gonna really build some serious muscles with this pile of books every day!'

He just laughed and handed me half the books.

Over the next four years, Kyle and I became best friends. When we were seniors, we began to think about college. Kyle decided on Georgetown and I was going to Duke. I knew that we would always be friends, that the miles would never be a problem. He was going to be a doctor, and I was going for business on a football scholarship.

Kyle was valedictorian of our class. I teased him all the time about being a nerd. He had to prepare a speech for graduation.

I was so glad it wasn't me having to get up there and speak. Graduation day, I saw Kyle. He looked great. He was one of those guys who really found himself during high school. He filled out and looked good in glasses. He had more dates than I had, and all the girls loved him. Boy, sometimes I was jealous.

Today was one of those days. I could see that he was nervous about his speech. So, I smacked him on the back and said, 'Hey, big guy, you'll be great!'

He looked at me with one of those looks (the really grateful one) and smiled. 'Thanks,' he said.

As he started his speech, he cleared his throat, and began. 'Graduation is a time to thank those who helped you make it through those tough years. Your parents, your teachers, your siblings, maybe a coach... but mostly your friends. I'm here to tell all of you that being a friend to someone is the best gift you can give them. I'm going to tell you a story.'

I just looked at my friend with disbelief as he told the story of the first day we met. He had planned to kill himself over the weekend. He talked of how he had cleaned out his locker, so his Mom wouldn't have to do it later and was carrying his stuff home. He looked hard at me and gave me a little smile.

'Thankfully, I was saved. My friend saved me from doing the unspeakable.'

I heard the gasp go through the crowd as this handsome, popular boy told us all about his weakest moment. I saw his Mom and dad looking at me and smiling that same grateful smile. Not until that moment did, I realise the depth or what I had accomplished that day.

He ended his speech by saying, *'Never underestimate the power of your actions. With one small gesture you can change a person's life.'*

Is your child a bully?

Here are some signs that your child might be a bully:

- Complaints from school about your child's behaviour;
- Seems to have unaccountable money;
- Complaints from other parents about their behaviour;
- Buys things that you know they can't afford;
- Explanations that their friends gave them the designer clothes they're wearing;
- Have a cocky, superior air about them.

School Hazing

Years ago, it was common to have hazing of junior students at the beginning of a school year. Most of the pranks revolved around being the servant of an older student for a day, but lately, that hazing has taken a dangerous turn and students have been seriously hurt, maimed or even killed when pranks go amiss.

One Canadian student died when the senior students forced their 'slaves' to consume raw hard liquor. One boy was forced to drink a half bottle of vodka until he passed out. When students couldn't revive him, they called for an ambulance. The boy barely survived the ordeal.

Stalkers:

Studies show that the overwhelming number of stalkers are male, and the overwhelming number of their targets are females.

A teen who loses a girlfriend may turn into a stalker, just so he can keep up the illusion that everything is still okay. Intimate partner stalkers refuse to believe that the relationship has ended. Most of these stalkers are not lonely people who are still hopelessly in love. On the contrary, they have been emotionally abusive and controlling both during and after the relationship has ended.

The only thing one should say to the stalker is 'No' once only, and then never say anything to him/her again.

If the stalker cannot have his target's love, s/he will settle for his/her hatred or his/her fear. The worst thing in the world for stalkers is to feel they're being ignored.

Delusional stalkers frequently have had little, if any, contact with their targets. Another more tenacious type might believe that s/he is destined to be with someone, and that if s/he only pursues him/her hard enough and long enough, s/he will come to love him.

The vengeful stalker is driven by vengeance, rather than love. They become angry with their targets over some slight - either real or imagined. This could be anger at another teen getting a higher mark on a test than they or feel that a person stole his/her best friend from him/her.

What parents can do to help a bullied child

When a parent finds out his or her child has been bullied, the initial feelings are of outrage and anger and their first reaction is to act and take steps to stop the bullying. But what are they to do?

If the child is physically injured, these would need to be attended to first. If possible, take coloured photos of the injuries and/or any damage there may be to the child's clothing or belongings. Sympathise with the child and let him/her know that this is a case of bullying and you will be taking steps to stop it from happening again. Interview any witnesses. If the injury is serious, lodge an assault case with the police against the bully. If the child is afraid to have you say anything, explain that if s/he does nothing, it protects the bully who is counting on the child not to 'tattle.'

Write down all the details about the incident - what happened, where it happened, who was involved and names of any witnesses. If the bullying took place on school property, speak with the school principal and give a copy of your written notes about the bullying incident. Add the school's reactions to your complaint, giving name of person, staff position, date and time of interview. Schools have a legal responsibility to ensure that they will provide a non-violent environment for all students.

Contact the parents of the bully. Many will co-operate, but others don't see the bullying actions as being important enough to deal with it. In the latter homes, violence and abuse are usually the normal behaviour so the parents will not be concerned about doing something to stop the bullying.

Point out that there was physical damage (either to the child or his/her possessions) and that what has happened is assault. Explain that you'll be reporting it to the school, and it could become necessary to contact the police. Let them know you're serious about your complaint and what you expect them to do:

- Have the bully apologise to your child;
- Determine what punishment the child will have for the bullying incident and what they'll do if the incident happens again;
- Warn the child that if this behaviour happens again, that you will go to the police and charge them with assault.

Parents of a bullying child need to ask themselves whether their actions to each other in the home have contributed to their child believing that bullying is acceptable behaviour.

If the school or parents do not show that they'll deal with and stop the bullying, go higher in the school system. If this doesn't prove successful, send a copy of the report of all events to date to the police for their files and advise them that you're seeing a lawyer. If you can't afford a lawyer, low cost legal aid is available in most cities.

When a child is enrolled in a school, the parents should ask for copies of school policies relating to bullying; how many incidents have taken place in the past few years and what steps they should take if an incident takes place. They should insist that they be informed of all bullying incidents that occur that affect their child (whether the child was a target, a bully or a witness).

Anti-Bullying Policies

Many schools have an unofficial reputation for tolerating bullying. This reputation is usually common knowledge throughout the student community. In these schools more children tend to feel anxious about their personal safety and as a result many are reluctant to go to school.

To tackle bullying you will have to liaise closely with the school and will probably have to talk to the bully's parents. Establish first whether this is an isolated incident (in which case nipping it in the bud is likely to have a high probability of success) or whether the child bully has a history of bullying behaviour.

Remember that most children will try bullying at some time. Most will soon realise that it's not an appropriate way of behaving and grow out of it quickly, especially if you help your child see why it's inappropriate and encourage and support them in learning better ways of behaving.

Only when the issue of bullying is brought into the open and policies and procedures showing how the school will deal with bullying are widely known *and enforced* will schools gain a reputation for being safe for *all* children.

Even students who can't be categorised as targets or bullies, but who might witness bullying, feel more comfortable when they know that the school stands against bullying. When children know that the school, they attend has a 'zero tolerance' to bullying and have an Anti-Bullying plan in force, they can then concentrate on their studies.

When they enter a school with a Zero-Tolerance for bullying, students who have bullied before usually test the policy. Transferring student's records should be examined to see if there were any bullying incidents at their last school. If there were notations about bullying, the zero-tolerance school must instruct new students about the school's bullying policies and procedures. School faculty must maintain a high profile in terms of the behavioural expectations of their students to gain support and trust from the students.

A commitment by the staff to no-bullying in the school must be a long-term undertaking.

Schools can crate support groups where targets can concentrate on developing coping skills needed to change their place within the social hierarchy. The goal is for the target to become a part of the group of students who do not bully and are not bullied. Such changes require a great deal of time and effort, but it's possible, given the necessary support of parents, schools and the community at large.

Students are key to a successful Anti-Bullying campaign primarily because they usually know who the bullies are long before the adults do. They're more likely to support an Anti-Bullying campaign if they're directly involved in determining the need for such a program and its implementation. This includes developing anti-Bullying policies and subsequent school-wide activities with instructions on what should be done if bullying is witnessed.

School authorities need to make students feel that teachers will ensure that the information they share will not cause them to lose status in their peer group. Confidentiality must be maintained so the program must be seen by the students as workable. Students need to understand the differences between ratting and reporting incidents.

'Ratting' occurs when a student tells about an inappropriate act with the idea of getting another student into trouble.

'Reporting' happens when a student tells to protect the safety of themselves or another student.

Once students understand the difference between the two, reporting bullying incidents becomes much less of a social taboo.

Each school should have a clearly written school behaviour policy that includes school bullying and hazing. There should be clear boundaries between what is acceptable and what is not. It should be linked to a system of rewards for good behaviour and should promote respect of others and intolerance of bullying behaviour. Those who do not follow the policy should receive counselling on how to raise their self-confidence level in other ways than bullying others.

Bullies will be shown how they can be more self-disciplined and empathetic and know what the consequences will be should their behaviour not fit the school behaviour policy. They must know that there is a zero-tolerance to bullying at the school and that there are severe consequences for unacceptable behaviour.

Australian Anti-School Bullying Policies

Australia has a multitude of excellent anti-school bullying programs available. The question is - why is school bullying increasing and becoming far more violent - rather than decreasing?

If these programs were effectively implemented, there would be far less bullying in our schools. Only a coordinated effort of our government, the departments of education, the schools themselves, the police, the entire community and parents, will we stamp out school bullying! I believe that the Federal Government Department of Education should put in place anti-bullying policies and procedures that should be used in *every* school in Australia. This way, consistency would be kept, and all children would be protected. That policy should include professional counselling for both the bully and the bullied, until their behaviour is stabilised.

When you consider that fifty-six per cent of Victorians aged eleven to twenty-one (surveyed by the Sunday Herald Sun) reported being targets of schoolyard bullying - and sixty-nine per cent in the eleven to fifteen age group - these programs need the help of the entire community to change bullying.

Sports Idols

Our children are constantly exposed to violence - and I don't just mean watching gun battles and murder scenes on the television. Have you really paid attention to what they're watching in our sports-addicted society? If you have, you'll notice how much aggression and violence is now used in the name of 'sport.' Grown men poke other players, gouge bodies, and generally act the part of the school bully.

And we wonder why our children clone that behaviour! Our society needs to look seriously at cleaning up the violence, drug use and criminal activity we now see in several of our sports. Sport used to be 'sportsmanlike' but the violent actions we see in our football players - can not be called sporting at all.

Sports Bullying

A recent report by UNICEF released in Italy on violence in sport, said nearly one in ten Australians had suffered sexual abuse in a sporting context. Sexual violence against children in sport in Australia could be as high as 8 per cent compared to Canada, where 2.6 per cent of children reported experiencing unwanted sexual touching.

Trisha Layhee, one of the report's authors said the rates of sexual violence may be much higher and work was needed to assess the issue. Dr. Layhee, who now heads the Hong Kong Sports Institute, said Australia was unique in the world for having a coaching culture that encouraged extreme psychological abuse.

'What we found was the complete normalisation of psychologically abusive behaviour by coaches, particularly at the elite level. I mean coaches screaming at kids,' Dr. Layhee said.

Her survey of 370 elite and club athletes in Australia found 31 per cent of female and 21 per cent of male athletes reported sexual abuse under the age of 18. Of these, 41 per cent of females and 29 per cent of males said the abuse occurred in a sporting context.

Once listed in the Swimming Queensland Hall of Fame, Scott Volkers was stripped of that honour following evidence given at the royal commission into child abuse. A trio of his swimming stars, Julie Gilbert, Kylie Rogers and Simone Boyce claimed they were abused as children while being trained by Volker's training squad in the 1980s and 1990s. He is also being investigated to see if there are enough grounds for the Queensland Director of Public Prosecutions to lay charges against him over the alleged sexual abuse. Mr. Volkers has denied all allegations of wrongdoing.

Chapter 4
Cyber Bullying:

What is Cyber bullying?

Cyber bullying is any harassment that occurs via the Internet. Vicious forum posts, name-calling in chat rooms, posting fake profiles on web sites and mean or cruel e-mail messages are all ways of cyber bullying.

Cyber bullying is threatening, lying about, stalking or otherwise harassing a person on-line or via other electronic communication devices like a cell phone. It is becoming a bigger problem as more and more people spend time on the Internet. There are several behaviours that are considered cyber bullying, including:

- Sending harassing messages;
- Impersonating another person and gaining trust;
- Posting someone else's personal information;
- Posting false or unsavoury information about another person;
- Posting private or doctored pictures about another person;
- Using the Internet to encourage others to bully the target.

Cyber Bullies (and other bullies such as school and workplace bullies) use these behaviours:

- Are very controlling of others. If someone resists, they're vicious in their attack to regain that control;
- They don't listen to others, lack conscience, show no remorse, are drawn to power, are emotionally cold and flat, dysfunctional, disruptive, divisive, rigid and inflexible, selfish, insincere, insecure, immature and lack interpersonal skills;

- They are vicious, criticising and vindictive in private - but charming in front of witnesses. (Others often don't see this side of their nature);
- Are very convincing or compulsive liars and when called upon, can fabricate authentic-sounding reasons for their behaviour;
- Are charming and convincing, which they use to make up for their lack of empathy;
- Hiding under their charming exterior is often sexual harassment, discrimination and racial prejudice;
- On the surface they seem very self-assured, but inside they're very insecure people;
- They excel at deception - have vivid imaginations - are often very creative;
- They encourage feelings of shame, embarrassment, guilt and fear - for that is how all abusers, including child sex abusers, control and silence their targets;
- When others describe their uncaring nature, they respond with impatience, irritability and aggression;
- Often have an overwhelming, unhealthy and narcissistic need to portray themselves as being a wonderful, kind, caring and compassionate person; in contrast to their behaviour and treatment of others;
- Are oblivious to the discrepancy between how they like to be seen (and believe they are seen) and how they are seen;
- Are unaware of leadership qualities (maturity, decisiveness, assertiveness, trust and integrity) and bullying (immaturity, impulsiveness, aggression, distrust and deceitfulness);
- Show inappropriate attitudes to sexual matters or behaviour;

- Refuse to acknowledge, value or praise others;
- When called upon to account for their actions, they aggressively deny everything and then counter-attack with distorted or fabricated criticism and allegations. If this is insufficient, they quickly feign being the target, often bursting into tears (the purpose is to avoid answering the question and thus evade accountability by manipulating others using guilt).

Who are the targets of the cyber bullies?

It is often assumed that targets of bullying are weak and inadequate. Targets of bullying are assumed to be loners, but most are independent, self-reliant and have no need for gangs or cliques. They have neither a need to impress nor are they interested in putting others down. Bullies select individuals who prefer to use dialogue to resolve conflict and who will go to great lengths to avoid conflict. The targets constantly try to use negotiation rather than resorting to grievance and legal action. Targets are chosen because they're competent and popular. Bullies are jealous of the easy and stable relationships targets have with others.

A key factor in the bully's choice is any child who is unwilling to resort to violence to resolve conflict - in other words, a child who has integrity and good moral codes. Given that bullies are driven by jealousy and envy, any child who is bright and popular is also likely to be targeted.

Parents, teachers and carers must ensure that these children know how to deal with bullying. Once bullying starts, many children will side with, or appear to side with the bully because they know that otherwise they themselves will be bullied.

The bully is a deeply unpopular child with whom other children associate, not through friendship, but through fear.

Many studies that show bullies to be popular, fail to make this distinction. Also, the education system is biased towards physical strength (i.e. undue emphasis on sport and rewards for sporting achievement) while artistic achievements are undervalued. Children who are bullied tend to be imaginative, creative, caring and responsible. Children who bully are unimaginative, uncaring, aggressive, emotionally immature, inadequate (especially in social skills) and irresponsible.

There is a lot anecdotal evidence to suggest that the child who learns to bully at school, *and gets away with it,* then goes on to be the serial bully in the workplace. A key factor in the bully's choice is any child who is unwilling to resort to violence to resolve conflict - in other words, a child who has integrity and good moral codes.

By the time a person enters adulthood at around the age of 18, their behaviour patterns are set and only time or a traumatic experience can alter these patterns. However, people who are likely to be bullied have a considerable learning capability and thus have a greater capacity to modify their behaviour as an adult. People who are bullies are prone to having limited learning capacity (especially in interpersonal and behavioural skills) and will often exhibit bullying behaviours for the rest of their lives.

Emotionally, the bully remains a young child and their attention-seeking behaviour is characteristic of a two-year-old throwing a temper tantrum to gain attention. Serial bullies have psychopathic or sociopathic tendencies that include a learning blindness and an apparent lack of insight into their behaviour and its effect on others.

What are the results to the target of bullying?

- The targets' constant high stress level interferes with their immune system causing frequent illnesses such as the flu, ulcers, irritable bowel problems, skin problems such as eczema, psoriasis, athlete's foot, shingles, colds, coughs, ear, nose and throat infections;
- Their bodies' batteries never have an opportunity to recharge;
- They suffer from aches and pains in the joints and muscles or have back pain with no obvious cause that won't go away or respond to treatment;
- They're disempowered such that they become dependent on the bully to allow them to get through each day without their life being made a hell;
- Initially they're reluctant to act against their bullies and report them knowing that they could accelerate the abuse. Later this gives way to a strong urge to act against the bullies so that others don't have to suffer a similar fate;
- In the workplace, many targets are so traumatised by the bullying that they need professional help or take stress leave until the incidence of bullying is investigated. Bullies love this because they can claim that their target is "mentally ill" or "mentally unstable" or has a "mental health problem." It's much more likely that this allegation is a projection of the bully's own mental health problems which have not been treated;
- For the targets that become victims of abuse, their world and self-view is shattered, and they may find it impossible to function normally or effectively. Research would indicate that often those who suffer most from unacceptable abusive behaviour are those

with the most to give - those with high expectations of themselves and those who are prepared to go the extra mile because they believe that what they do is meaningful and important.

The targets' behaviour:

- An overwhelming desire for acknowledgement, understanding, recognition and validation of their experience and strong motivation for justice to be done;
- An unwillingness to talk or interact with the bully;
- An unusually strong sense of vulnerability, victimisation or persecution;
- An unusually strong desire to educate the public and help the public introduce bullying prevention laws;
- An overwhelming sense of betrayal and an inability or unwillingness to trust anyone;
- Headaches and migraines;
- Shattered self-confidence and low self-esteem;
- Became seriously depressed, especially upon waking;
- Became tired, exhausted and lethargic;
- Found their levels of guilt were abnormally high which precluded them from starting new relationships;
- Found themselves constantly fatigued (like Chronic Fatigue Syndrome) or sweated, trembled, shook or had heart palpitations;
- Suffered from panic attacks triggered by any reminder of the experience;
- Impaired memory that was due to suppressing horrific memories;
- Physical numbness (toes, fingertips, lips) and emotional numbness (especially the inability to feel joy);
- Constantly been on alert because their fight or flight mechanism had become permanently activated;

- Found they're constantly on edge mentally – had a short fuse and were irritated, especially by small insignificant events;
- Often been highly upset by the amount of anger they felt towards their abuser and were horrified by the mental pictures of creative, cruel, torturous ways they could pay back their abuser;
- Found that going to school became difficult, often impossible to undertake;
- Became hypersensitive and inappropriately perceived almost any remark as critical;
- Became obsessed with the abusive experience that took over their lives, eclipsing and excluding almost every other interest;
- Believed that their abusive problems are hopeless and that their efforts to stop the situation will be futile;
- Been sleepless, had nightmares, constantly reliving events, woke early or woke up more tired than when they went to bed;
- Poor concentration and became forgetful especially with trivial day-to-day things;
- Experienced regular intrusive, violent visualisations and flashbacks and couldn't get the abuse out of their minds;
- Became emotional - bursting into tears regularly over trivial matters;
- Became uncharacteristically irritable, had angry outbursts, were hypersensitive and felt fragile;
- Had feelings of withdrawal and isolation, wanted to be on their own and sought solitude;
- Suffered from post-traumatic stress disorder (PTSD).

The four stages of fear

Targets often go through four stages of fear when faced with anything that appears dangerous to them:

1. **Arousal** – their muscles tense, breathing and heart rate increase;
2. **Fight or Flight** – the body's automatic defence response when dealing with threat;
3. **Freezing/Immobility** – the above response is put on hold, they freeze and become unable to respond or escape from the threat;
4. **Dormant Immobility** – a rest state once the threat has passed.

Animals are generally able to return to their normal mode of functioning as soon as the danger passes, but humans often can't and may become locked into a recurring pattern of the above responses.

If the cyber bullying is threatening, children should be advised to immediately stop logging onto the site and tell their parents, a teacher, Crime Stoppers or the police.

Cyber bullying is usually not a one-time communication, unless it involves a death threat or a credible threat of serious bodily harm. In extreme cases people have killed each other or committed suicide after being involved in a cyber bullying incident.

Children need to be reminded that if they are bullied – they're not at fault – the person doing the bullying is at fault and will be charged accordingly.

Examples of bullying

- A student is bombarded by anonymous threatening and taunting e-mails at home, even though there is no direct harassment at school.

- The target has no idea who is sending the messages and starts to feel like everybody is against him/her. That student is being cyber bullied.
- A school bulletin board is spammed with name-calling posts that spread vicious rumours about a specific student. The rumours aren't true, but kids at school see the posts and believe them. The student is then excluded by other peers. This student is the target of cyber bullying.
- A nasty fake profile is posted at a social networking site using a student's real name, photo, and contact information. That student starts getting weird e-mail messages from strangers who think the profile is real. Some of the messages are crude. Some of the messages are mean. This is another example of cyber bullying.

These are just a few examples of cyber bullying. If you are taking part in things like this – it's not harmless fun. You're being a cyber bully. If you are the target of this type of treatment you are being cyber bullied and there are things you can do to stop the harassment.

How common is cyber bullying during the teen years?

Bullying is not new but thanks to the Internet teens are now being bullied at home. On-line harassment, more often called cyber bullying, is a serious problem. When bullying comes home via the Internet it can leave targets feeling helpless and overwhelmed.

Parents should know a few cyber bullying facts before their preteens begin middle school. About one in five teens reports being targeted by cyber bullying, according to a comprehensive study of nine- to eleven-year-olds. The researchers found that eleven percent of children had been targeted on-line or through their cell phones one or two times in the previous year.

An additional ten percent of the students had experienced cyber bullying three or more times in the year.

Additional cyber bullying facts: When asked about the form of the bullying, eighteen percent of the targeted teens said that the bullying happened through e-mail while seventeen percent said it occurred in a chat room. Bullying via instant messages was less common (thirteen percent), as were text messages (twelve percent), comments on a website (eleven percent), and distribution of an embarrassing photo (seven percent).

Most of the targeted teens said they did not know the form the cyber bullying took (twenty-five percent) or reported that it took a different form than any of the forms listed here (twenty-two percent). These findings indicate how much researchers still must learn about cyber bullying. The unclear results about forms of cyber bullying also underscore the secrecy and shame that often accompany being bullied.

Why Do People Cyber bully?

Some bully because their role models (often their parents or older siblings) are also bullies. It's natural for children to mimic the behaviour of their role models. Others seem to be born with a lack of empathy towards others or a feeling that they're superior to others. It's almost impossible for these individuals to understand what their bullying behaviour does to their targets. Only professional counselling (sometimes lasting for years) can reverse these flawed individuals.

Bullying has been around forever, but cyber bullying is different because it lets a bully remain anonymous and thanks to the Internet, teens are now being bullied at home. It's easier to bully in cyberspace than it is to bully face to face. With cyber bullying a bully can pick on people with much less risk of being caught.

Bullies are natural instigators and in cyberspace, bullies can enlist the participation of other students who normally may not be willing to bully in the real world. Unfortunately, kids who stand around doing nothing in a real-life bullying incident often become active participants in on-line harassment.

The detachment afforded by cyberspace makes bullies out of people who would never become involved in a real-life incident. The Internet makes bullying more convenient and since the target's reaction remains unseen people who wouldn't normally bully don't take it as seriously.

What Can Be Done About Cyber bullying?

There are many things that can be done to combat cyber bullying.

Remember the bullies in high school when we were young? Cyber bullying is a new way to bully and crops up out of our teens' ability to connect with each other through internet social websites, e-mail and cell phones. While the ability to talk with friends in these different ways is fun, it has given bullies a new way of doing what they want to do - hurt people. And that is the main point I want to make here: Using the internet to bully is new, but bullying isn't.

Therefore, if your teen is dealing with cyber bullying, you treat it just as you would if your teen is being bullied in the school yard. Here are some tips on what you can do if your teen is dealing with cyber bullying.

Preventing Cyber Bullying

Teaching children to respect others and to take a stand against bullying of all kinds helps and they should be rewarded for taking that stand. Schools can work with parents to stop and remedy cyber bullying.

They can also educate the students on cyber ethics and the law. If schools are creative, they can sometimes avoid the claim that their actions exceeded their legal authority for off-campus cyber bullying actions.

Educating the kids about the consequences (losing their ISP or IM accounts) helps. Teaching them to respect others and to take a stand against bullying of all kinds helps too. Because their motives differ, the solutions and responses to each type of cyber bullying incident must differ too. Schools can work with parents to stop and remedy cyber bullying.

Parents also need to understand that a child is just as likely to be a cyber bully as a target of cyber bullying and often go back and forth between the two roles during one incident. They may not even realise that they're seen as a cyber bully.

1. **Set rules.** Parents need to make it a part of their computer rules or parenting contract that their teen will show them any threats, or any type of hateful words made to them. They'll also want to stress to their teen that they will not tolerate them saying things that are hurtful to others.
2. **Teach your teen to be savvy with their social networking.** Show your teen how to delete offending messages and block cyber bullies from being able to leave messages on their social websites.
3. **Tell your teen it's okay not to 'friend' everyone** who asks on Facebook or other social network sites.

How you can stop Cyber Bullying once it starts

There are two things parents must consider before anything else.

- Is their child at risk of physical harm or assault?
- How are they handling the attacks emotionally?

If there's any indication that personal contact information has been posted on-line or any threats are made to their child, they must run, not walk, to their local law enforcement agency.

Take a print-out of all instances of cyber bullying to show them but note that a print-out is not enough to prove a case of cyber harassment or cyber bullying. You'll need electronic evidence and live data for that. It's crucial that all electronic evidence be preserved to allow the person to be traced and to take whatever action needs to be taken. The electronic evidence is at risk of being deleted by the Internet service providers unless you notify them immediately that you need those records preserved! So, check to see which e-mail account they came in on and phone the Internet service provider.

Parents need to be the ones students trust when things go wrong on-line and/or offline. Yet students often don't go to their parents. Why? Because their parents tend to over-react. Most children will avoid telling their parents about a cyber bullying incident fearing they will only make things worse.

Unfortunately, sometimes parents also under-react. They need to be supportive of their children and realise that these attacks can follow them into their otherwise safe home and wherever they go on-line. The risk of emotional pain is very real and very serious, so parents should not ignore their plight.

Why is cyber bullying so serious?

It may seem like cyber bullying is a trivial matter. You might think the answer is to just ban them from going on-line or stop them from opening their messages, hoping everything will blow over.

Even if you believe that in-person bullying is a problem, it might seem like there's little damage that can be done on-line. This is far from the truth, however. Cyber bullying can be even more dangerous than in-person incidents:

- It can be more difficult to stop an on-line bully;
- Emotional violence can be more damaging than physical violence;
- Cyber bullying can have long term effects as gossip, lies, photos and videos stay long after bruises fade;
- Cyber bullying follows people into the home, which would normally be considered a haven from this type of activity;
- It's easy to impersonate another person on-line, gain someone's trust and then turn on them.

Penalties for Cyber Bullying

Although targets might lodge criminal charges, most of the time the cyber bullying does not go so far that the law must intervene, although targets often might attempt to lodge criminal charges. Cyber bullying, however, may result in a misdemeanour cyber harassment charge, or if the bullying child is young enough may result in the charge of juvenile delinquency. It must have a minor on both sides, or at least have been instigated by a minor against another minor for this to happen.

It typically can result in the person losing their ISP or IM accounts because s/he violated his/her terms of service rules. In some cases, if hacking or password and identity theft is involved, they can be charged with serious criminal charges by state and federal law enforcement agencies.

Unfortunately, many do not report cyber bullying or don't know who to talk to about the bullying.

Because the cyber bully's motives differ, the solutions and responses to each type of cyber bullying incident must differ as well. We encourage schools to work with parents to stop and remedy cyber bullying and educate students about cyber ethics and the law.

Deal with Cyber Bullying when it happens

The most important thing a target of cyber bullying can do is not respond to the bully.

- Don't play into the bully's games;
- Don't answer e-mails!
- Don't respond to posts!
- Don't engage in a chat room exchange;
- Don't copy what the bully is doing!
- Ignore the bullying and get help from parents and teachers;
- Don't ignore cyber bullying. Ever. Explain to your teen that it's not their fault they were targeted by a cyber bully. Often teens turn these problems inward and start to feel far less confident about themselves. Verbally affirm that they're not at fault and they'll be less likely to take a hit to their self-esteem level;
- Don't get involved in the cyber bulling and don't let your teen prolong it. The more you or your teen try to talk to whomever is doing the bullying, the more it will escalate, and you could be found at fault for not reporting the problem in the first place;
- If your teen is cyber bullied at school, report the incident to the school. Include a screen shot or copy of the e-mail where the cyber bullying took place. If the school is unable to do anything, report the incident to the police;

- Also, be sure to report the incident to your internet service. If the cyber bullying incident takes place while your teen's at home, report the incident to the ISP of the offender by forwarding the e-mail or reporting it to the site it occurred on;
- If the cyber bullying includes threats of physical violence, report them to your local police *immediately*. This may seem harsh, because it's an e-mail and the person is not right there now, but a physical threat of violence is nothing to take lightly. Protect your teen. You should especially report it to the police if it continues for any length in time and is not just a one-time incident;
- If the cyber bullying is happening anonymously, *it's even more important to report it.* It may never turn into something violent, but many times it does. The police can track down who's sending the e-mails - so let them handle it;
- While you will ignore the bully, be sure to save the evidence, so that school officials, Internet providers and even the police can properly deal with the bully. Cyber bullying may give bullies anonymity, but it always leaves evidence and a trail of information that can be checked out by experts.

Can Cyber bullying be stopped?

Schools must take all types of bullying seriously. As soon as the cyber bullying starts, go to school officials for help. Ask to see their policy about bullying and cyber bullying because cyber bullying is often an extension or escalation of bullying that's already happening at school. If this is the case, ask what has been done to stop the bullying. Parents should be kept informed about what's happening now and what has happened in the past.

The police are unlikely to become involved if the bullying is limited to a few isolated incidents or a couple of mean e-mails or instant messages. However, if you get even one communication that includes a threat of bodily harm or a death threat the police should be alerted immediately.

About twenty youths across Queensland take their lives each year. Most are between fifteen and seventeen years-of-age, but suicides of children aged ten to fourteen have increased. Content on on-line forums such as Facebook and Tumbir heighten the risk of copycat suicides where users urge others to take their own lives or harm themselves.

Be aware that others urging people to commit suicide is considered a death threat and the police will treat it accordingly.

Vulnerable children who've been bullied or have mental health issues are at risk. Parents need to carefully monitor what happens to them on social media or texting on their phones.

Why is Cyber Bullying so difficult to stop?

- Traditional bullies might be suspended from school, banned from certain places or activities or even arrested, but cyber bullies are more elusive;
- The anonymity of the Internet makes it difficult to be sure who's doing the bullying;
- The anonymity of the Internet makes cyber bullies (especially kids) bolder;
- Cyber bullying can cross state and even international lines, making it nearly impossible to prosecute;
- Most cyber bullies may think they won't get caught or punished;
- Others may play down the damage the cyber bully is doing.

When should the police become involved?

Repeated or excessive harassment via e-mail, forums or chat rooms is harassment and should involve the police. Threats of violence should be reported to the police. Be sure to save all messages as evidence. The police will know what to do with them.

Don't put up with cyber bullying; get help. Cyber bullying leaves a clear trail of evidence and this can work to the advantage of the target. Cyber bullies are just bullies with a new weapon in their arsenal of harassment, so treat them like you would any bully and they lose their power.

How to prevent your child from being targeted

Be your child's support system.

The biggest way to prevent your child from being a target is to keep the lines of communication open. This means walking a fine line between a concerned caregiver and an overprotective parent. Your child needs to feel that s/he can come to you without negative repercussions. If they're afraid you'll ban them from using the Internet or keep them from going out with friends, they will not confide in you. It also means listening carefully and avoiding the tendency to trivialise what they're experiencing. It may not seem like a big deal to an adult that the most popular kids in school made fun of your child's hair or clothes, but it can be a serious blow to the self-esteem of a child or teen if that happens.

Be firm.

Set rules regarding when and how long your child can be on-line. Accessing the Internet is akin to inviting someone into your home, so you may choose to only allow Web time when you're at home. Use Internet filters, timers, and whatever else you need to do to protect your child.

Know your child.

This is very important. Kids who are already suffering from low self-esteem or depression are prime targets for cyber bullying. It can be tempting to assume that your child is just going through a phase or that they're just in a 'bad mood,' but you're better off seeking professional help if there's a problem rather than simply waiting things out.

Know the danger signs.

Your child may become more withdrawn or moody. S/he may spend more time online or may refuse to use the computer altogether. They may cut off ties with friends. If your child gives any indication that they are being bullied on or offline, take it seriously.

Educate.

Teach your child what to do in cases where they feel threatened or bullied. They should ignore the offender and contact an adult immediately. They should never engage with the person who's threatening them as that will only encourage the behaviour to continue. As an adult, if you feel threatened by someone on-line, contact the police just to be safe. You can also use built-in measures on certain websites, such as ignoring or reporting someone else.

Chapter 5
The New Synthetic Drugs

An excellent video about the new synthetic drugs can be found on Youtube: *Crime Stoppers Queensland - New Synthetic Drugs: Real Damage - Doctor Interview*
https://www.youtube.com/watch?v=xp0_aWr77t4

What are Synthetic Drugs?

The term synthetic drugs is often used to describe drugs that are new to the market or have become more widely used in recent years. The effect of these drugs mimics those of more established drugs like LSD, cocaine and cannabis but are sometimes much more potent.

The name 'synthetic drugs' can be confusing, because it doesn't distinguish these newer drugs from illicit drugs such as LSD, ecstasy and speed that are also synthesised from chemicals (rather than extracted from plants like cannabis, cocaine and heroin).

These new drugs can be ordered legally over the internet mainly from China where the drugs are legal. Producers of these substances have been traced back to factories in China that are selling them on the web. They're shipped by courier and seem to be able to slip under the radar of custom officials because of their packaging.

They're cheap and are sold as 'legal highs.' Locally, convenience stores, sex shops and tobacco shops are innocently selling the drugs, not knowing that they're causing horrific results. There have been many deaths and users (some of them very young) suffer from terrible health problems such as strokes, heart damage, kidney/renal damage where some must go on dialysis. Others have violent outbursts, psychosis, irrational fears and depression.

Some are so depressed that they commit suicide. Others must drop out of school because they can't think straight.

Over one hundred of these new synthetic drugs are being sold and as one is banned, another one appears with a slightly different chemical makeup. Some are marketed in little packets that resemble collector cards of sports legends and many parents don't know what they really are.

They can be packaged as party pills, powders, herbal highs, bath salts, teas or even plant food, but often contain new but untested chemicals designed to mimic the effects of drugs like cannabis, LSD and amphetamines.

They have names such as: OMG, Tai High, Kryp2nite, Rave, Blueberry, Smacked, Kapow, Amsterdam Royal, K2, Black Mamba, Spice, Benzo Fury, Kronic, Minga and White Revolver.

The one that has caused innumerable deaths – *251-NBome (i.e.: N-Bomb) is twenty-five times stronger than LSD.*

These are hallucinogens – that is, drugs that distort perceptions – and both can cause psychosis (a loss of contact with reality) in certain people. Others aren't even aware they're taking NBOMe because they think they're buying LSD.

When one substance in Australia is banned, the legal process takes so long that there's plenty of time for another drug to take its place. The Ministry of Health have estimated that $140 million of these drugs sold over just 10 months.

These synthetic drugs can have other toxic effects on the body not experienced with LSD including seizures, agitation, heart and blood vessel problems, hypothermia, metabolic acidosis (the kidneys can't remove enough acid from the body) organ failure and even death.

One teenager took one of these drugs, began talking a mile a minute, running around in circles, had a terrible panic attack and jumped off a balcony to his death.

Synthetic Cannabis

Another drug that's deadly is the synthetic cannabis that is *one hundred times stronger than marijuana*. Synthetic cannabis is essentially plant material that has been sprayed with chemicals and can cause irreparable kidney damage.

People smoke these products, so they can experience a *'high'* like marijuana. It's been associated with an increasing number of deaths and serious adverse effects.

Some people have also experienced severe mental health effects including hallucinations, psychosis, panic and anxiety after taking synthetic cannabis. Although they're popular among young people (especially teenagers) evidence suggests they are also popular with adults in their twenties and thirties. A 2011 survey of 316 users of synthetic cannabis products found that fifty per cent of users were aged twenty-eight and over and a quarter were over thirty-five.

Mephedrone

Another drug rearing its ugly head is cheaper than ice and has a devastating effect on users and appeals to those who use methamphetamines. This drug is mephedrone, a type of amphetamine which causes hallucinations, aggressive and bizarre behaviour, hypertension and can lead to death.

The synthetic drug trade has invaded our youth and we're having a terrible time keeping these drug dealers from hurting our youngsters. Some of the people selling these synthetic drugs are earning up to thirty thousand dollars a day, so it's hard to discourage them from selling them when the profits are so good. There's a new counterculture that exploits the legal loopholes that give users a mind-altering high by changing the chemical makeup of synthetic drugs to keep ahead of what the police can do to stop them.

Spice was the earliest in a series of synthetic cannabis products sold in many European countries. Since then several similar products have been developed, such as Kronic, Northern Lights, Mojo, Lightning Gold, Lightning Red and Godfather.

The Australian government has imposed a blanket ban on possession or selling substances like alcohol, tobacco and food that have substantially the same effect as a dangerous drug. However, stores throughout Australia are still openly selling illicit psycho-active drugs which mimic marijuana, cocaine, LSD and ecstasy. Some of these drugs have up to one hundred times the active ingredient in illicit drugs such as cannabis, making users guinea pigs and crash-test dummies, while the criminals rake in the profits.

Sex shop owners and tobacco shops are still the main suppliers, despite new laws banning their sale. Synthetic cannabis is sold as a tea for eighty dollars for a three-gram packet. These special teas are dipped in a potentially fatal hallucinogenic substance that has led directly to the deaths of youngsters.

Our biggest problem is that we don't know what's in many of these drugs – but we do know the results – organ failure, seizures, and paranoia.

Community-minded people are encouraged to report seeing any of these drugs before someone else ends up in an emergency ward of a hospital or die.

At the end of May 2015, a drug derived from cannabis lost its status as a poison in Australia and will be included on the list of prescription-only medications. Trials of medicinal cannabis are expected to begin in 2015 in Queensland, NSW and Victoria. Cannabis itself remains illegal in all states of Australia.

How can harm from these drugs be reduced?

Be aware of the following (some of this advice comes from the Australian Drug Foundation):

Note: EPS is short for 'emerging psychoactive substances.' (The term psychoactive means the drugs affect the brain causing changes in thought, mood and/or behaviour).

- Because products are constantly changing, it's very hard to determine the effects of EPS, even if the person has taken them before. So, activities like driving, swimming and operating machinery are especially unsafe for anyone affected by these drugs.
- Many EPS contain a range of fillers and numbing agents that could lead to health problems, particularly if injected.
- Some products can cause seizures and/or fast or irregular heartbeats. These are especially problematic if the user has any underlying health conditions.
- Given the large number of these drugs on the market, it can be difficult for medical practitioners to know how to treat someone who has overdosed on or has health problems caused by EPS. Treatment could be quicker and more effective if someone could advise exactly what has been taken and the dosage. Supplying the packet might be helpful.

If someone is badly affected by any drug, call an ambulance straight away. Don't let fear of police involvement affect your decision. Waiting a few hours can make the difference between someone being saved or being dead.

Ambulance officers will not call on police to be involved unless there is a death, serious violence where they need help controlling the situation, or if the person has illicit drugs on them when they arrive at a hospital.

New idea for ensuring a party-goer's drugs are safe

Two countries are tackling the drug situation in a unique way – and other countries are seriously looking at it because it seems to be working. Establishments where they know the patrons are using drugs – are setting up a pill analysis to tell the owner whether the drug is safe to take. The person remains anonymous – but is given a number when they leave their pills with the tester. Half an hour later the drug user returns to the testing site and is informed whether the drug is safe. If the drug is too potent for the weight of the user, the testers will suggest that the owner take one quarter or one-half of the pill rather than a full pill that could have dangerous after-effects. For some pills, the owner is advised that there are dangerous chemicals in the pills, and they should not take them. The owner of the drugs leaves the testing area with his/her drugs.

In Austria and The Netherlands experts are running these drug-checking services. Studies of Austria's program (which has run for over two decades) show that one-third of the people who had their drugs tested, decided not to take them; proving that drug-checking services reduced drug use - rather than increased it.

There's a big difference in the way people use ecstasy in Australia compared to Europe and often they don't have an idea of the real contents of what they're taking. That lack of knowledge, combined with Australia's position as the largest per-capita users of ecstasy in the world, is a recipe for disaster. This drug testing might be the answer.

However, NSW Drugs Squad Commander Tony Cooke explained that he doesn't think drug-checking will ever be allowed in Australia because that would be a 'tacit support' of drug use, and 'these drugs are illegal.'

Many would think that this new concept will only encourage drug use but banning the drugs doesn't seem to be working and some think it's an alternative to seizing the drugs, arresting and jailing the users (who will leave jail and continue buying more drugs).

Smoking during and after pregnancy

Another danger to children is their parents' own addiction to smoking – both cigarettes and marijuana.

Parents who smoke either cigarettes or marijuana when they're around children are child abusers. Second-hand smoke diminishes the blood supply to the bones and cuts off vital nutrients and contains up to 150 times higher levels of carcinogens than smoke directly inhaled by cigarette smokers.

The most vulnerable passive smokers are babies in the womb. With every puff, the amount of blood and oxygen going to the foetus is decreased. This is what creates brain damage. Five minutes after the mother has a cigarette, her baby's heart speeds up and breathing movements decrease. These are signs of foetal distress.

The mother's risk of having a stillborn baby is significantly increased and she is eighty percent more likely to have a spontaneous abortion than a non-smoker. If she smokes, her baby's body and brain will weigh less at birth and its chances of mental retardation and birth defects, such as port wine stain, cleft palate and harelip, will be higher.

Many researchers have found that the dreaded sudden infant death syndrome is passive smoking-related. A shocking estimate is that twenty to thirty per cent of Australian women smoke during their pregnancies, affecting 76,500 babies born in Australia every year.

Chapter 6
Illicit Drugs

Chroming

What are the short- and long-term effects of inhalant use?

Most inhalants produce a rapid high that resembles alcohol intoxication, with an initial high followed by drowsiness, loss of inhibition, lightheadedness, and agitation. These effects may include belligerence, apathy, impaired judgment, dizziness, drowsiness, slurred speech, lethargy, depressed reflexes, general muscle weakness, nausea and vomiting. It can affect functioning in work, school or social situations; nausea. Research shows that toluene can produce headache, euphoria, giddy feelings, and the inability to coordinate movements. Exposure to high doses can cause confusion and delirium. If sufficient amounts are inhaled, nearly all solvents and gases produce anesthesia - a loss of sensation - that can lead to unconsciousness.

Inhaled nitrites dilate blood vessels, increase heart rate, and produce a sensation of heat and excitement that can last for several minutes. Other effects can include flush, dizziness, and headache.

Many individuals report they have a strong need to continue using inhalants, particularly those who have abused inhalants for prolonged periods over many days. Inhalant users on average, start smoking cigarettes, drink alcohol, and try almost all other drugs at younger ages and display a higher lifetime prevalence of substance use disorders, including abuse of prescription drugs.

The highly concentrated chemicals in solvents or aerosol sprays can induce irregular and rapid heart rhythms and lead to fatal heart failure within minutes of a session of prolonged sniffing. This syndrome, known as "sudden sniffing death," can result from a single session of inhalant use by an otherwise healthy young person. Sudden sniffing death is associated particularly with the abuse of butane, propane, and chemicals in aerosols. Inhalant abuse also can cause death by:

Asphyxiation - from repeated inhalations that lead to high concentrations of inhaled fumes, which displace available oxygen in the lungs;

Suffocation - from blocking air from entering the lungs when inhaling fumes from a plastic bag placed over the head;

Convulsions or seizures - from abnormal electrical discharges in the brain;

Coma - from the brain shutting down all but the most vital functions;

Choking - from inhalation of vomit after inhalant use; or

Fatal injury - from accidents, including motor vehicle fatalities, suffered while intoxicated.

© *Australian Drug Foundation 2014.* Used with permission - See more at:
http://www.adf.org.au/legal-miscellaneous/australian-drug-foundation-copyright-requests#sthashZAdBXstZ.dpuf

Inhalants

- **National:** 3.8% of Australians aged fourteen years and over have used inhalants one or more times in their life[1].
- 0.8% of Australians aged fourteen years and over have used inhalants in the previous twelve months[1].
- **Young people:** Young Australians (aged fourteen to twenty-four) first try inhalants at 16.9 years of age on average[1].
- Around one in five twelve to seventeen-year olds have deliberately sniffed inhalants at least once[9].

- **Victoria:** In 2012/13 the number of ambulance attendances related to inhalant use in metropolitan Melbourne dropped by 10% - from 135 in 2011/12 to 122 in 2012/13. Attendances in regional Victoria increased by 121% - from fourteen to thirty-five years of age[10].

Alcohol

- **National:** Alcohol is the most widely used drug in Australia.
- 86.2% of Australians aged fourteen years and over have drunk alcohol one or more times in their lives[1].
- 37.3% of Australians aged fourteen years and over consume alcohol on a weekly basis[1].
- The age group with the greatest number of Australians who drink daily is seventy plus years[1].
- Around one in five (18.2%) Australians over fourteen drink at levels that put them at risk of alcohol-related harm over their lifetime[1].
- Around one in six (15.6%) people aged twelve years or older had consumed eleven or more standard drinks on a single drinking occasion in the past twelve months[1].
- One in four women drink alcohol while pregnant, even though the Australian Alcohol Guidelines recommend not drinking during this time[1].
- $7b is generated by alcohol-related tax. But alcohol costs society $15.3b annually[3].
- Alcohol caused more than twice as many deaths (3,494) than road accidents (1,600) in 2005[4].
- One in ten workers say they have experienced the negative effects of a co-worker's use of alcohol[5,6].
- **Young People:** Young Australians (aged fourteen to twenty-four) have their first full serve of alcohol at 15.7 years on average[1].

- 72.3% of twelve to seventeen-year-olds have not consumed alcohol in the last twelve months[1].
- 17% of fifteen to eighteen years old say they had sex when drunk which they later regretted[7].
- Alcohol contributes to the three major causes of teen death: injury, homicide and suicide[8].
- Friends or acquaintances are the most likely sources of alcohol for twelve to seventeen-year-olds (45.4%), with parents being the second most likely source (29.3%)[1].
- **Victoria:** On average, there were thirty alcohol-related ambulance attendances in metropolitan Melbourne per day in 2012/13 (25% increase from 2011/12), and ten per day in regional Victoria (30% increase). The average age of these patients was forty years[10].
- Alcohol was the reason for most drug-related ambulance attendances, with 11,159 attendances in 2012/13 compared to 3,159 for benzodiazepines, 1,901 for heroin, 1,584 for non-opioid analgesics (such as paracetamol) and 1,112 for crystal methamphetamine (ice)[10].

Analgesics

- **National:** 7.7% of Australians aged fourteen years and older have used analgesics for non-medical purposes one or more times in their life[1].
- 3.3% of Australians aged fourteen years and over have used analgesics for non-medical purposes in the previous twelve months[1].
- **Young People:** Young Australians (aged fourteen to twenty-four) first try analgesics for non-medical purposes at fifteen years on average[1].
- Analgesics are the most commonly used drug (licit or illicit) among twelve to seventeen-year olds. By the age

of thirteen, 95% of this age group have used analgesics (mostly for headaches and/or cold and flu symptoms)[9].
- 4% of twelve to seventeen-year olds take analgesics from home without permission and 3% buy them[9].
- **Victoria:** The number of opioid analgesic ambulance attendances in 2012/13 increased significantly compared with the previous year – 55% increase in metropolitan Melbourne and 21% in regional Victoria. There was also an increase for non-opioid analgesics – 38% in metropolitan Melbourne and 34% in regional Victoria[10].
- Non-opioid analgesics (such as paracetamol) are the third most common drug involved in ambulance attendances, following alcohol and benziodiazepines[10].

Benzodiazepines

- **National:** 4.5% of Australians aged fourteen years and over have used tranquillisers/sleeping pills (including benzo-diazepines) for non-medical purposes one or more times in their life[1].
- 1.6% of Australians aged fourteen years and over have used tranquillisers (including benzodiazepines) for non-medical purposes in the previous twelve months[1].
- **Young people:** Young Australians (aged fourteen to twenty-four) first try tranquilisers for non-medical purposes at 18.2 years on average[1].
- **Victoria:** Benzodiazepines contributed to fifty-six deaths in Victoria in 2010, representing almost 17% of the total number of drug-related deaths investigated by the Coroners Court of Victoria in that year[11].
- In 2012/13 there was an average of eight ambulances attendances per day for benzodiazepines in metropolitan Melbourne, and two per day in regional Victoria. Both represent small increases from the previous year. The

average age of the patients involved in these attendances was thirty-eight to forty years[10].
- Benzodiazepines are the second most common drug involved in ambulance attendances in Victoria, after alcohol[10].

***Betel nut*:** Around 10–20% of the world's population chews betel nut in some form. This makes it the fourth most widely-used psychoactive substance, after nicotine, alcohol and caffeine[12,13].

Cocaine

- **National:** 8.1% of Australians aged fourteen years and over have used cocaine one or more times in their life[1].
- 2.1% of Australians aged fourteen years and over have used cocaine in the previous 12 months[1].
- **Young people:** Young Australians (aged fourteen to twenty-four) first try cocaine at 19.2 years on average[1].
- The 1.7% of twelve to seventeen-year olds who take cocaine have only used it once or twice[9].

Caffeine (including energy drinks)
- In Australia between 2004 and 2010, there were 297 calls to the NSW Poisons Information Line concerning toxicity from caffeinated energy drinks. The most commonly reported symptoms included palpitations/tachycardia, tremors, shaking, agitation and restlessness.[27]
- **Consumption:** One billion cups of coffee per year were consumed at cafés, restaurants and other outlets in Australia in 2006[26].
- Consumption of coffee has doubled over the past thirty years from 1.2 to 2.4 kg per person in Australia[26].
- Global coffee consumption increased in 2010, with consumers spending a total of $10.7 billion, which is

equivalent to 2.4 kilograms of coffee per person, per year[28].
- Sales of energy drinks in Australia and New Zealand increased from 34.5 million litres in 2001 to 155.6 litres in 2010[29].

Cannabis

- **National:** 34.8% of Australians aged fourteen years and over have used cannabis one or more times in their life[1].
- 10.2% of Australians aged fourteen years and over have used cannabis in the previous twelve months[1].
- **Young people:** Young Australians (aged fourteen to twenty-four) first try cannabis at 16.7 years on average[1].
- 14.8% of twelve to seventeen-year olds have tried cannabis – it is the most commonly used illicit drug among this age group[9].
- **Victoria:** There were 3.88 cannabis-related ambulance attendances in metropolitan Melbourne per day and 1.52 in regional Victoria in 2012/13. The average age of the patients involved in these attendances was thirty years[10].
- Between 2011/12 and 2012/13, there was a 10% increase in the number of attendances for cannabis in metropolitan and regional Victoria that resulted in hospital transportation[10].
- Ambulance attendances for cannabis continue to rise, with more than double in 2012/13 than in 2003/04 in metropolitan Melbourne[10].

Ecstasy

- **National:** 10.9% of Australians aged fourteen years and over have used ecstasy one or more times in their life[1].
- 2.5% of Australians aged fourteen years and over have used ecstasy in the previous 12 months[1].

- **Young people:** Young Australians (aged fourteen to twenty-four) first try ecstasy at 18.2 years on average[1].
- 2.7% of twelve to seventeen-year olds have tried ecstasy[9].
- **Victoria:** In both metropolitan and regional Victoria, there was an over 60% increase in the number of ambulance attendances where the patient believed they had taken ecstasy between 2011/12 and 2012/13[10].
- The proportion of attendances where the patient reported having ecstasy and alcohol decreased by 10% in metropolitan Melbourne[10].
- The number of attendances resulting in hospital transportation increased in 2012/13, which could indicate an increase in harmful substances being included in ecstasy pills[10].

GHB

[GHB (gamma hydroxybutyrate) is a depressant drug that slows down the messages travelling between the brain and body. Other names G, fantasy, grievous bodily harm (GBH), liquid ecstasy, liquid E, liquid X, Georgia Home Boy, soap, scoop, cherry meth, blue nitro. GHB is usually swallowed, but sometimes it's injected or inserted anally.]

- **National:** 0.9% of Australians aged fourteen years and over have used GHB one or more times in their life[1].
- **Young people**
- Young Australians (aged fourteen to twenty-four) first try GHB at 20.1 years on average[1].
- **Victoria:** The number of GHB ambulance attendances in 2012/13 increased by 42% (up to 578 attendances) in metropolitan Melbourne and 3% (42) in regional Victoria from the previous year[10].

Hallucinogens

- **National:** 9.4% of Australians aged fourteen years and over have used hallucinogens one or more times in their life[1].
- 1.3% of Australians aged fourteen years and over have used hallucinogens in the previous twelve months[1].
- **Young people:** Young Australians (aged fourteen to twenty-four) first try hallucinogens at 18.5 years on average[1].
- 3% of twelve to seventeen-year olds have tried hallucinogens such as LSD[9].

Heroin

- **National:** 1.2% of Australians aged fourteen years and older have used heroin one or more times in their life[1].
- 0.1% of Australians aged fourteen years of age and older have used heroin in the previous twelve months[1].
- **Young people:** Young Australians (aged fourteen to twenty-four years of age) first try heroin at 16.9 years on average[1].
- 1.6% of twelve to seventeen-year olds have tried heroin[9].
- **Victoria:** There were 5.21 ambulance attendances related to heroin in metropolitan Melbourne and 0.28 in regional Victoria per day in 2012/13 (these numbers include non-fatal overdose)[10].
- There was a 13% decrease in the number of ambulance attendances for heroin overdose in metropolitan Melbourne and 15% decrease in regional Victoria in 2012/13 compared to the previous year[10].

Naloxone

- Naloxone successfully reversed twenty-three opioid overdoses between 2011 and 2013, during a peer administration trial in Canberra[14].
- In Australia in 2009, there were 563 accidental deaths attributed to opioids among people aged 15-54 years. In the over fifty-five age group, there were seventy deaths. Many of these deaths were due to multiple drugs being taken including prescription opioids[15].

Methamphetamine (including ice)

- **National:** 7.0% of Australians aged fourteen years of age and over have used meth/amphetamines one or more times in their life.[1]
- 2.1% of Australians aged fourteen years of age and over have used meth/amphetamines in the previous twelve months. Of these people, 50.4% report crystal or ice as main form of the drug used.[1]
- **Young people:** Young Australians (aged fourteen to twenty-four) first try meth/amphetamines at 18.6 years on average[1].
- 2.9% of twelve to seventeen-year olds have tried amphetamines[9].
- **Victoria:** The daily number of all amphetamine-related ambulance attendances in 2012/13 increased significantly compared with the previous year – 88% increase in metropolitan Melbourne and a 198% in regional Victoria. This is attributed to an increase in the number of attendances relating to crystal meth-amphetamine (ice).[10]
- In metropolitan Melbourne there was an 88% increase in the number of attendances for ice (crystal methamphetamine) between 2011/12 and 2012/13, up to

an average of three per day. In regional Victoria, the increase was 198%, up to 0.63 per day[10].
- Ice (crystal methamphetamine) is the fourth most common drug involved in ambulance attendances, following alcohol, benziodiazapines and non-opioid analgesics (such as paracetamol)[10].

New psychoactive substances

New psychoactive substances (NPS) are being developed at an unprecedented rate. The European Monitoring Centre for Drugs and Drug Addiction (EMCDDA) and Europol currently monitors more than 450 NPS, which is close to double the number of substances controlled under the United Nations international drug control conventions. More than half of these have been reported in the last three years [16].

- **National:** 0.4% of Australians aged fourteen years and over have used new psychoactive substances at some stage in their lives[1].
- 0.4% of Australians aged fourteen years and over have used new psychoactive substances in the previous twelve months[1].
- **United Kingdom:** In the UK, there has been an increasing trend in NPS deaths with sharp increases between 2011 and 2012 (twenty-nine to fifty-two deaths). The number of deaths involving NPS rose again in 2013 by 15% to sixty deaths[17].

Nitrous Oxide

According to the Australian Trends in Ecstasy and Related Drug Markets 2013 Survey one quarter (25%) of the sample reported recent nitrous oxide use in the six months preceding the survey. This is comparable with 2012 results. Use was highest in Victoria (45%)[31].

Pharmacotherapy drugs

(methadone, buprenorphine and naloxone)

On a snapshot day in June 2012, 46,697 clients were receiving pharmacotherapy treatment in Australia. 68% received methadone, 19% received buprenorphine–naloxone and 13% received buprenorphine.[23]

Oxycodone

- **National:** The amount of oxycodone being prescribed by doctors increased from 95.1 kg in 1999 to 1270.7 kg in 2008 – a thirteen-fold increase[18].
- **Victoria:** The amount of oxycodone being prescribed by doctors increased nine-fold from 7.5 mg per capita in 2000 to 67.5 mg per capita in 2009[18].

Synthetic cannabis

An on-line study recently conducted in 2012 found that of the people who use the drug:
- The median age is 27 years;
- 70% are male;
- 78% are employed;
- 7% use daily;[20]
- **National:** 1.3% of Australians aged fourteen years and over have used synthetic cannabis at some stage in their lives[1].
- 1.2% of Australians aged fourteen years and over have used synthetic cannabis in the previous twelve months[1].
- According to Australian data from the Global Drug Survey, synthetic cannabis was the twentieth most

commonly used drug – 4.1% of respondents had used this type of drug in the last twelve months[20].

Tobacco

- **National:** 39.8% of Australians aged fourteen years and over have used tobacco[1].
- More males than females are daily smokers across all age groups[1].
- People who smoke aged twelve years and over smoked on average 95.9 cigarettes per week[1].
- Around one in eight (12.8%) Australians aged fourteen years and over smoke daily[1].
- In 2012, 12.5% of all mothers reported that they had smoked while pregnant. This is down from 13.2% in 2011 and 13.5% in 2010[30].
- Teenage mothers accounted for 10.2% of all mothers who reported smoking during pregnancy. But of all teenage mothers, 34.9% reported smoking[30].
- **Young people:** Young Australians (aged fourteen to twenty-four) have their first full cigarette at 15.9 years on average[1].
- 77% of twelve to seventeen-year olds have not smoked. The proportion of twelve to seventeen-year olds who have never smoked decreases in the older age groups, but by age seventeen more than half have still never smoked[9].
- Around 4% of all twelve to seventeen-year olds have smoked more than one hundred cigarettes in their lifetime, which peaks at 9% among seventeen-year olds[9].

Overdose

In Australia in 2009, there were 563 accidental deaths attributed to opioids among people aged fifteen to fifty-four years. In the over fifty-five age group, there were seventy deaths. Many of these deaths were due to multiple drugs being taken including prescription opioids. Alcohol and other drug experts suggest that opioid-related deaths in Australia are increasing.[21]

Of all illegal substances, heroin and other opioids were involved with the largest number of drug-related deaths, despite the number of people using them being low compared to other substances. Amphetamines including 'ice' have the second highest death rate of illegal drugs.[22]

References
1. Australian Institute of Health and Welfare. (2014). Canberra: AIHW.
2. Callinan, S., & Room, R. (2012). *Alcohol consumption during pregnancy: results from the 2010 National Drug Strategy Household Survey*. Canberra: Foundation for Alcohol Research and Education.
3. Manning, M., Smith, C., & Mazerolle, P. (2013). *The societal costs of alcohol misuse in Australia*. Canberra: Australian Institute of Criminology.
4. Collins, D., & Lapsley, H. (2008). *The costs of tobacco, alcohol and illicit drug abuse to Australian society in 2004/05*. Canberra: Commonwealth of Australia.
5. Laslett, A.M., Catalano, P., Chikritzhs, T., et al. (2010). *The range and magnitude of alcohol's harm to others*. Fitzroy: AER Centre for Alcohol Policy Research.
6. Dale, C.E., & Livingston, M. (2010). The burden of alcohol drinking on co-workers in the Australian workplace. *Medical Journal of Australia, 193*(3), 138-140.
7. Smith, A., Agius, P., Mitchell, A., Barrett, C., & Pitts, M. (2009). *Secondary students and sexual health 2008: Results of the 4th National Survey of Australian Secondary Students, HIV/AIDS and Sexual Health*. Melbourne: Australian Research Centre in Sex, Health and Society.

8. National Health and Medical Research Council. (2009). *Australian guidelines to reduce health risks from drinking alcohol*, Canberra: NHMRC.
9. White, V., & Bariola, E. (2012). *Australian secondary school students' use of tobacco, alcohol, and over-the-counter and illicit substances in 2011.* Melbourne: The Cancer Council, Victoria.
10. Lloyd, B., Matthews, S., & Gao, C.X. (2014). *Ambo Project – Alcohol and drug related ambulance attendances: Trends in alcohol and drug related ambulance attendances in Victoria 2012/13.* Fitzroy: Turning Point Alcohol and Drug Centre.
11. Coroners Court of Victoria. (2012). *Finding into death with inquest, Inquest in the Death of David Andrew Trengrove*, Delivered on 18 May 2012.
12. World Health Organization. (2012). Geneva: World Health Organization.
13. Ashock, L., Deepika, N., Sujatha, G.P., & Shiva P.S. (2011). 'Areca nut: To chew or not to chew?'. *e-Journal of Dentistry*, *1*(3), 46–50.
14. Olsen, A., McDonald, D., Lenton, S., & Dietze P. (2014). Canberra: ACT Health.
15. Roxburgh, A., & Burns, L. (2013). Sydney: National Drug and Alcohol Research Centre (NDARC).
16. European Monitoring Centre for Drugs and Drug Addiction (EMCDDA). (2015). New psychoactive substances in Europe – An update from the EU Early Warning System, Lisbon: EMCDDA.
17. Office for National Statistics. (2014). 2013 Newport: Office for National Statistics.
18. Rintoul, A.C., Dobbin, M., Drummer, O.H., & Ozanne-Smith, J. (2011). Increasing deaths involving oxycodone, Victoria, Australia, 2000-09. *Injury Prevention*, *17*(4), 254–259.

19. Barratt, M.J. (2012)., Melbourne: Yarra Drug and Health Forum.
20. Global Drug Survey. (2014). London: Global Drug Survey.
21. Roxburgh, A., & Burns, L. (2013). Sydney: National Drug and Alcohol Research Centre (NDARC).

[Author's note: In 2013 the number of Australians being treated for codine addiction had tripled to more than 1,000 a year, up from 318 in 2003. An intake of eighty tablets a day can cause significant damage to organs. In 2010, a spike in people abusing the painkillers sparked a supply change where products such as Nurofen Plus, Panadeine and Panadeine Extra were sold in smaller packs and issued by pharmacists.

The most used drug in the 1960s was diazepam but was available only from the person's GP.

Crystal Methamphetamine

Crystal methamphetamine (Ice) use in Australia is almost eight times the US level and almost five times the UK Level. Users spend an average of $300 to $500 per day feeding their habit and two-thirds admitted they committed crime to pay for it. Young people are turning to ice as a cheaper alternative to alcohol.

Ice lasts longer than LSD, cocaine, ecstasy and speed. A single hit floods the brain with dopamine making the person feel elated, alert and focused. However, the regular and huge bursts of dopamine that at first made the person feel great, wears out the pleasure-producing regions of their brain and they begin to feel depressed and agitated at the same time.

A new danger is being identified for those who move into homes that were Meth Labs. If properties formerly used for the clandestine manufacture of methamphetamine are not properly cleaned, the public might be unknowingly exposed to drug residues. A family of five moved into a home that was previously a methamphetamine drug laboratory. The family developed adverse health effects. Based on hair samples, there was evidence of absorption of methamphetamine from the environment. Adverse health effects were most pronounced in the youngest child, who also had the highest methamphetamine levels in his hair, possibly related to a combination of repeated contact with surfaces during play activities and less frequent hand washing.

Appropriate identification and management of these properties, including measures by authorities to prevent the sale of these homes, are important to prevent exposures and adverse health effects.

'Meth Mouth' has cost Australians $1 million plus for prisoner's dental work in the past year. Stimulants such as methamphetamine cause 23% of those costs resulting in stained or rotting teeth. People in their 20s are losing all their teeth.

Here are some examples of the devastating results of using Ice:

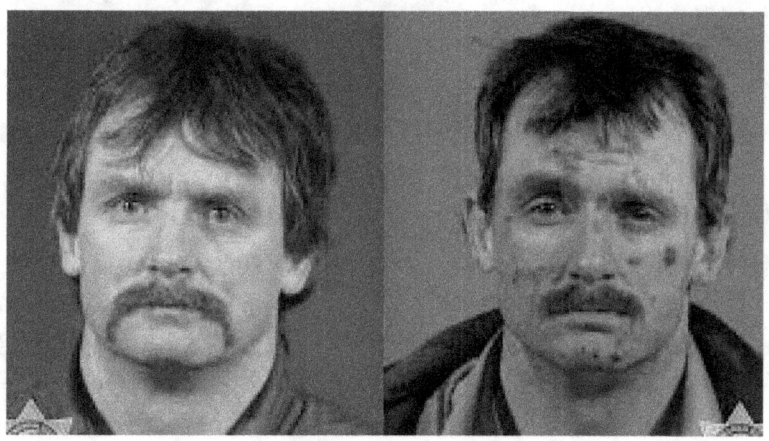

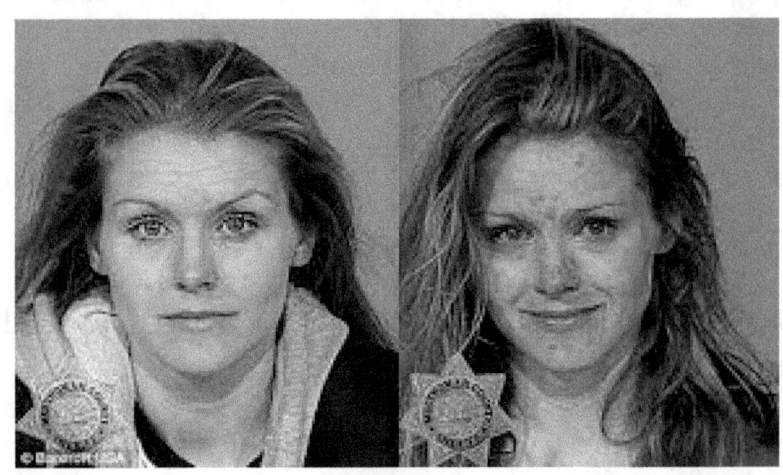

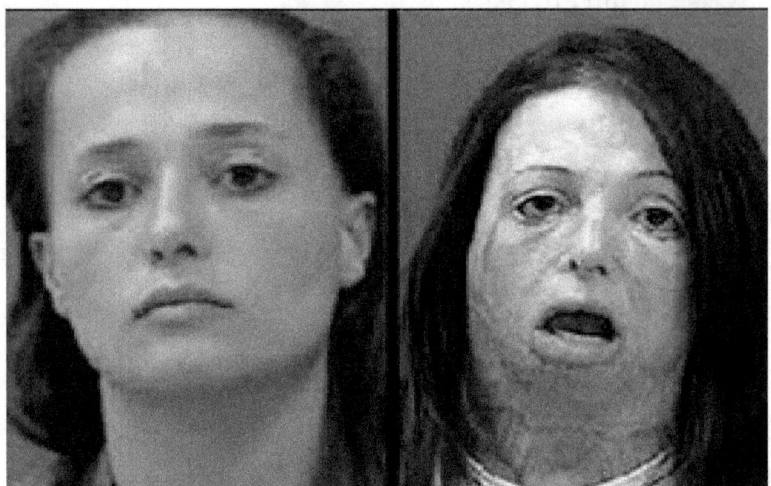

The woman in this set of pictures was 27 years old in the first photograph and 30 years old in the second.

Heather Raybon was left permanently scarred with terrible facial burns after being caught in a blast at a meth lab in 2004. Police in Florida said that despite the life-changing incident, the 31-year-old has continued to try to manufacture crystal meth. She has undergone numerous facial surgeries in the past seven years.

The third picture shows how she looked seven years later.

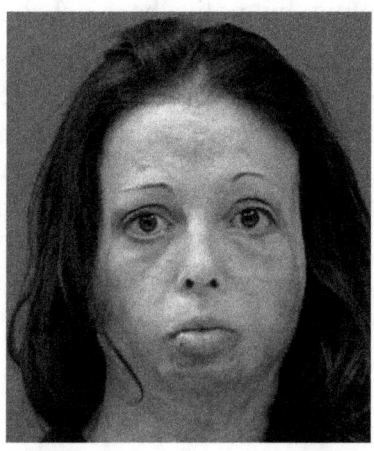

Ice users now account for nine out of ten people seeking help from some drug services. Ice addicts usually lose weight because they may not sleep or eat – just smoke ice with a glass pipe day and night. They lose teeth and their bodies become covered with drug sores.

Ice is a stimulant drug, which means it speeds up the messages travelling between the brain and the body. It's a type of methamphetamine, which is generally stronger, more addictive and has more harmful side effects than the powder form known as speed.

In Australia one 14-year-old Ice-addicted girl living in Brisbane costs the state $12,000 a week for her care, because she refuses to stop using Ice and keeps running away to earn money to buy more drugs.

Former NSW premier Neville Wran's daughter Harriet Wran was arrested on August 13, 2014 accused of murdering a drug dealer. She battled an addiction to ice before her arrest.

Murder of Phil Walsh

Adelaide Crows coach Phil Walsh was murdered in July 2015 by his son Cy Walsh, 26. It's thought the drug ice was a factor in the killing, but police have not commented.

Cy was apprehended and placed in a high-security mental facility after being charged with the murder of his father and the stabbing of his mother Meredith in the leg. Phil was attacked in his bed and was stabbed multiple times in the back. Cy fled on foot but was apprehended shortly after. His court date is set for September 15, 2015.

Chapter 7
Teen Depression and Suicide

If there's a downside to the teen years, it must be moody behaviour. Emotional development and the teen years aren't easy for teens or parents. As your child faces increasing pressure at school, socially, and faces confusion and anxiety over puberty, you can expect plenty of mood swings. For girls, mood swings may be sparked by hormonal changes before or during menstruation, rejection from peers, and increased pressures at school.

Mood swings can present themselves quickly and unexpectedly, but they are usually short lived. Moody teens often need time alone to calm down and put things into perspective. If your teen struggles with mood swings, help him/her find ways to deal with his/her emotions positively. Discuss what kind of things make him/her feel better and encourage him/her to do one of those things to relieve his/her anxiety. For instance, s/he could listen to music, read a book or spend time playing video games.

Why teens experience moodiness

When we stop to consider all that teens are going through emotionally, physically and socially, it's no wonder they have bouts of moodiness.

Their hormones begin to fluctuate as they move toward puberty and they feel emotionally unstable. Teens also lack the emotional development to fully control their moods and express exactly what they're feeling as they're feeling it. Many are dealing with an increased stress level. One minute they still want to be cared for and protected and the next they want to be treated and act like a full-grown, independent person. Combine those elements and it makes for some volatile moods.

As children gradually develop into teenagers, their emotional development will be as obvious as their physical development. Teenage depression is an issue which confronts many parents who wonder if their child is just having a bad day, or is this a sign of a more serious problem? What's been happening in the child's life? How does s/he normally handle stress and is this out of his/her normal behaviour?

Here's how you could prepare your child from having a bad day that could otherwise result in depression.

- **Ensure your child is prepared for tests:** Forgetting that your child had a test is probably the easiest way to ruin his/her school day. Help your child update a weekly calendar so that s/he (and you) know when tests will take place and when projects are due. Of course, your teen won't know if a pop quiz is on the calendar, but by helping teens keep up with their homework and by staying on top of their studies, they'll be in a good position for those surprise quizzes.
- **Help them deal with a bad day:** If your child's behaviour is out of the norm, simply ask, 'So, how was your day?' No matter how much preparation they do ahead of time, at some point your child will come home from school with a tale of woe. But you can do a lot to take your child's thoughts off his school troubles. For example, you should:
   o Truly listen to your child if s/he wants to talk;
   o Find a fun way to distract the teen from his/her problems. You could go for a bike ride or watch a little television together;
   o Help them troubleshoot their problems. If they're having problems with a subject, offer to tutor them, or find a tutor for them. If they're having issues with a friend, role play possible solutions that might help ease the situation;

- Leave them alone. Some teens need a little privacy or down-time if they've had a bad day. Give your child some space if that's what s/he needs;
- Contact the school. If you think your child's problem might be serious, contacting his/her teacher or guidance counsellor might be a good idea, especially if you think bullying, violence, drugs or other serious issues might be the problem;
- Consider their life outside of school. Be sure your teens have activities that they can turn to after school. Extra-curricular activities give children the chance to broaden their social circle and develop interests that have nothing to do with school. They're also a great distraction when your child needs to forget about a bad school day.

How to handle normal moodiness

So, if you think you're dealing with a case of normal teen moodiness - then how do you cope? Remember that your child is not out to torture you, but is struggling with a strange cocktail of hormones, emotional instability and social strife. Cut him/her a little slack. At the same time, know that it's never okay for children to hurt others with their actions, no matter what they're going through.

Help them develop their empathetic skills by explaining how their actions affect you or other family members. Avoid 'you' phrases like 'You're completely out of line when you complain about dinner.' Instead use 'I' phrases, like 'I felt hurt when you complained about the dinner that I spent time making.' Recognise that your child might not respond positively at that moment. Before long, though, their mood will swing back, and you'll be together on the couch yet again. Well, at least for a little while…

What are mood disorders?

Even though most teen mood changes are normal, mood disorders can and do crop up during these often-difficult years. Two common mood disorders are major depressive disorder and bipolar disorder. Both disorders involve periods of low mood, irritability, apathy, sleep problems, eating disturbances, fatigue and decreased concentration.

In bipolar disorder, these depressed periods alternate with periods of mania or hypomania (low-level mania) that include an elevated or irritable mood, sleeping less, talking more, being hyperactive and showing poor judgment.

Older adolescents or adults with bipolar disorder often have episodes of these moods that can last weeks or longer, but a child with bipolar might instead switch between the high and low states with much greater frequency.

Differences between moodiness and mood disorders

So how can you tell whether your child is suffering from a mood disorder or is simply being a teen? One key difference is impairment. Every teen sulks at times but take note of whether your teen's brooding is getting in the way of going to school, eating and sleeping, participating in sports or meeting up with friends. Is s/he basically living life the same way as always? If so, the moodiness is most likely normal. Keep an eye on your child's classmates and friends. How are they acting? What sorts of mood swings are they going through? Observing typical behaviour in their peer group can help you gain perspective on what's 'normal' - even though it might not be anything like what's normal for us adults! On the other hand, you should talk with your child's doctor if your teen expresses a great deal of distress, begins to disengage from the world, says s/he wants to 'disappear' or talks about suicide and/or to wants to hurt others.

How common are mood disorders?

You might think the mood disorders sound a lot like your moody teen. Though, these disorders are relatively rare, especially in the teen age group. Major depressive disorder strikes only about two to four percent of people under eighteen, becoming more common with increasing age. Bipolar disorder is extremely rare before puberty; only about 1.2 percent of teens have the disorder. That said, mood disorders too often go undiagnosed in youth, according to the Child and Adolescent Bipolar Foundation. We don't want to brush off a situation that could be serious.

Being excluded affects behaviour

Teens who were excluded for a short time in a laboratory setting changed their behaviours markedly. They acted less energetically and more impulsively than their peers. Social exclusion is a powerful experience because it targets our evolutionary needs for protection and group acceptance.

Mood changes due to exclusion

Being excluded can also lead to changes in mood. Targets of social exclusion have more negative feelings and have an increased feeling of anger and sadness compared to people who are not excluded.

Being moody is part of the teen years. One minute your teen is snuggling next to you on the couch, the next you're being told you're embarrassing them if you touch them in public. Sometimes the changes can be more extreme, with your teen brooding in their bedroom for hours on end. It's hard to know when moodiness is the normal by-product of growing up and when it signals something more serious.

How can you tell if your teen is depressed?

Stress, or more appropriately *'distress'* occurs when an individual believes that the demands or perceived demands of a situation outweigh his/her ability or perceived ability to cope with the situation. The coping mechanisms under challenge include those the teen needs to resolve the problem, be it emotional, familial, peer-pressure or school pressures.

From a psychological viewpoint, depression occurs when the individual feels his/her world is consistently unpleasant, punishing or deprives him/her of the opportunity for a positive and satisfying life. Their negative experiences may be compounded by feelings of being unable to change their situation - a process of learned helplessness.

Teens with depression expect and predict that their unpleasant and distressing experiences will continue. Guilt-ridden perceptions of being responsible for their own distress, either through the things they have done or not done, or negative thoughts about their inability to cope, add to the depressed feelings. The combination of a negative view of their lives, the expectation that it will continue, the self-criticism or self-blame for the situation, coupled with the inability to cope, are the characteristic psychological processes of depression.

All teens experience some torment in their lives. It's almost hard-wired in their brains and hearts. But depression is different. It's often almost incapacitating in its impact on a teenager. Some of the symptoms of teenage depression include:

- Sadness or hopelessness;
- Irritability, anger, or hostility;
- Tearfulness or frequent crying;
- Restlessness and agitation;
- Difficulty with concentration;

- Feelings of worthlessness and guilt;
- Changes in eating and sleeping habits;
- Withdrawal from friends and family;
- Loss of interest in activities;
- Lack of enthusiasm and motivation;
- Fatigue or lack of energy;
- Thoughts of death or suicide.

What should you do?

If you think your teenaged son or daughter may be suffering from depression, you need to act. Teenage depression can move quickly from bad to worse. Make sure that your teen does not develop suicidal feelings; if they do, you need to respond immediately.

Of all the complications of untreated depression; suicide is the most tragic. It has often been called 'a permanent solution to a temporary problem.' Depressed people who take their own lives do so because they're suffering unbearable psychological pain and perceive that there are no more options available to them. Physical pain can also trigger suicidal feelings, but pain with a psychological origin can be just as, if not more, intense.

Stress Breakdown

Stress breakdown differs from a nervous breakdown or mental breakdown that are the consequence of mental illness. Stress breakdown is a psychiatric injury, which is a normal reaction to an abnormal situation. The two types of breakdown are distinct and should not be confused. A stress breakdown is a natural and normal conclusion to a period of prolonged negative stress; the body is saying:

'I'm not designed to operate under these conditions of prolonged negative stress so I'm going to do something dramatic to ensure that you reduce or eliminate the stress.

Otherwise, my body may suffer irreparable damage and I must take action now.'

Dr. John T. O'Brien, consultant in old-age psychiatry at Newcastle General Hospital published a paper subtitled: *"Prolonged stress may cause permanent brain damage."*

A stress breakdown is often predictable, sometimes days or weeks in advance. The person's fear, fragility, obsessiveness, hyper-vigilance and hyper-sensitivity combine to evolve into paranoia. If this happens, a stress breakdown is only days or even hours away and the person needs urgent medical help. The risk of suicide at this point is heightened. Research says that young men are committing suicide at five times the rate as females.

Self-Harm

Self-harm is linked to abuse, unwanted pregnancy and parental divorce. One in seventeen children is believed to hurt or self-harm itself. Behind these children is often a family in distress. Self-harm is the intentional cause to harm one's own body. These include deliberate self-harm, self-injury, self-mutilation, self-abuse, self-wounding, self-inflicted violence, para-suicide, non-fatal act, and wrist cutting. All these definitions of self-harm cover the same actions:

- Cutting;
- Burning skin by physical means using heat;
- Burning skin by chemical means using caustic liquids;
- Punching hard enough to cause bruises;
- Head banging;
- Hair pulling from head, eyelashes, eyebrows and armpits;
- Poisoning by ingesting small amounts of toxic substances to cause discomfort or damage;
- Insertion of foreign objects;

- Excessive nail biting to the point of bleeding and ripping cuticles;
- Excessive scratching by removing top layer of skin to cause a sore;
- Bone breaking;
- Gnawing at flesh;
- Wound interference to prevent wounds from healing thus prolonging the effect;
- Tying ligatures around the neck, arms or legs to restrict the flow of blood;
- Medication abuse without intention to die;
- Alcohol abuse;
- Illegal drug use;
- Smoking.

Cutting and burning are among the most common forms of self-harm. Those who are smoking and drinking often believe they are not consciously harming themselves; but are taking part in a socially accepted lifestyle. It's only once these actions become excessive that problems can occur.

There is also a strong correlation between eating disorders and self-harm. This is because starvation, binge-eating and self-induced vomiting, overuse of laxatives and diuretics, are forms of self-harm, as are starvation, binge-eating and vomiting.

Who Commits Suicide?

Some distinction has been made between those who attempt suicide and those who carry out their suicide attempt. Suicide attempters are likely to be female and generally attempt suicide by taking an overdose of medication.

Suicide completers are more often male and tend to use more lethal means of ending their lives. Both genders, however, may fall within either of these groups. Suicide threats should *always* be taken very seriously. They are a serious cry for help.

The primary risk factor for those who complete their suicides are; major depression, substance abuse, severe personality disorders, male gender, older age, living alone, physical illness, terminal illness and other previous suicide attempts. Chronic pain and illness have also been associated with suicide.

Suicide is most prevalent among the young and the elderly. It's the leading cause of death amongst those aged fifteen to twenty-four. Among those young people who attempt suicide, eventually anywhere between 0.1 and 10% of these will complete the act.

The tragedy of a young person dying because of overwhelming hopelessness or frustration is devastating to family, friends, and community. Parents, siblings, classmates, coaches, and neighbours might be left wondering if they could have done something to prevent that young person from turning to suicide.

The reasons behind a teen's suicide or attempted suicide can be complex. Although suicide is relatively rare among children, the rate of suicides and suicide attempts increases tremendously during adolescence.

It's also thought that at least twenty-five attempts are made for every completed teen suicide.

Overdose using over-the-counter, prescription, and non-prescription medicine is also a very common method for both attempting and completing suicide. It's important to monitor carefully all medications in your home. Also, be aware that teens will 'trade' different prescription medications at school and carry them (or store them) in their locker or backpack.

Suicide rates differ between boys and girls. Girls think about and attempt suicide about twice as often as boys and tend to attempt suicide by overdosing on drugs or cutting themselves. Yet boys die by suicide about four times as often as girls, perhaps because they tend to use more lethal methods, such as firearms, hanging, or jumping from heights.

It can be hard to remember how it felt to be a teen, caught in that gray area between childhood and adulthood. Sure, it's a time of tremendous possibility but it also can be a period of stress and worry. There's pressure to fit in socially, to perform academically and to act responsibly and yet still want to fit in with peers.

Adolescence is also a time of sexual identity and relationships and a need for independence that often conflicts with the rules and expectations set by others.

Young people with mental health problems - such as anxiety, depression, bipolar disorder, or insomnia - are at higher risk for suicidal thoughts. Teens going through major life changes (parents' divorcing, moving, a parent leaving home due to military service or parental separation, financial changes) and those who are targets of bullying are at greater risk of suicidal thoughts.

Factors relevant to Teen Suicide

Factors that increase the risk of suicide among teens include:

- a psychological disorder, especially depression, bipolar disorder, and alcohol and drug use (in fact, approximately 95% of people who die by suicide have a psychological disorder at the time of death);
- feelings of distress, irritability, or agitation;
- feelings of hopelessness and worthlessness that often accompany depression;
- a previous suicide attempt;
- a family history of depression or suicide;

- emotional, physical, or sexual abuse;
- lack of a support network, poor relationships with parents or peers, and feelings of social isolation;
- dealing with bisexuality or homosexuality in an unsupportive family, community or hostile school environment.

Warning signs

Suicide among teens often occurs following a stressful life event, such as problems at school, a breakup with a boyfriend or girlfriend, the death of a loved one, a divorce, or other major family conflicts.

Teens who are thinking about suicide might:

- talk about suicide or death in general;
- previous suicide attempts;
- seek access to something they can kill themselves with;
- give hints that they might not be around anymore;
- talk about feeling hopeless or feeling guilty;
- pull away from friends or family;
- taking less care of their appearance;
- write songs, poems, or letters about death, separation, and loss;
- start giving away treasured possessions to siblings or friends;
- lose the desire to take part in favorite things or activities;
- are moody, withdrawn, anxious, agitated or sad;
- engage in risky behavior;
- increased use of alcohol or drugs;
- have trouble concentrating or thinking clearly;
- experience changes in eating or sleeping habits;

- engage in risk-taking behaviours;
- lose interest in school or sports;
- overly positive after a period of being down that may indicate they've made up their mind to end their own life and feels relief that this decision has been made;
- have feelings of helplessness, that they're worthless, feel trapped, depressed, irritable and have no sense of purpose or reason for living.

The Suicide Awareness/Voices of Education (SA/VE) Website lists the following danger signs of those contemplating suicide:

- Talking or joking about suicide;
- Statements about being reunited with a deceased loved one;
- Statements about hopelessness, helplessness, or worthless-ness. Example: 'Life is useless.' 'Everyone would be better off without me.' 'It doesn't matter. I won't be around much longer anyway.' 'I wish I could just disappear;'
- Preoccupation with death. Example: recurrent death themes in music, literature, or drawings;
- Writing letters or leaving notes referring to death or 'the end;'
- Suddenly, they appear happier or calmer;
- Loss of interest in things they care about;
- Unusual visiting or calling people they care about - saying their good-byes;
- Giving possessions away, planning, setting their affairs in order;
- Self-destructive behaviour (alcohol/drug abuse, self-injury or mutilation, promiscuity);
- Having several accidents resulting in injury. Close calls or brushes with death;

- Obsession with guns or knives;
- Risk-taking behaviour (reckless driving/excessive speeding, carelessness around bridges, cliffs or balconies, or walking in front of traffic).

Treatment

The person who's depressed enough to be thinking of suicide needs immediate professional help. Don't feel afraid to bring up the topic with your teen. Ask questions about their plans. Those who are passively suicidal or have only vague ideas of wanting to die should still be taken very seriously and arrangements should be made for them to see a psychiatrist. If your teen seems in immediate danger of a suicide attempt, call 000 or your local emergency hospital and ask for assistance. Because medication and therapy take some time to become effective, it may be necessary for your child to be hospitalised for his/her own protection.

During a crisis, don't leave them alone. Don't minimise their feelings. It's not important that the problem seems trivial or easily solved to you. What counts is how severe the problem seems to them. Don't treat your teen as if you think they're just seeking attention.

Suicidal behaviour is an indication of deep psychological pain. They're asking for your help; so be sure to give it now – not later when you might feel less rushed. Reassure your child that s/he is not a burden to you, and s/he is not weak if s/he has those feelings. Instead, praise him/her for having the courage to ask for help.

As alert as you may be for the signs of suicidality in your teen, it may be that they hide their feelings from you or feel afraid to approach you. If you believe that your child may be clinically depressed, you need to consider the following:

Talk About It.

The first and most important thing to do is open the lines of communication. Share your specific concerns with your teen. Mention specific behaviours rather than just being general. Express your desire for their happiness and ask them to talk. Take an active listening approach - listen for feelings and then reflect them back. If you haven't been communicating regularly with your teen, it may take some time for him/her to open up to you. Take whatever time is needed. You might want to consider going for a walk or taking a drive, so you can chat privately. Make the experience less intimidating for your teenager.

When you talk, make sure teens know:

- **You're not judging them.** You know things can be hard for them, and what they're feeling is important. Even if their feelings seem irrational to you, recognise that they're very real to your teen.
- **You will not lecture.** Your job as a parent is to listen, not to rush in with answers and direction. Explore his/her feelings without being critical or offering advice that may or may not be welcome.
- **You will support them.** If there are things your teen needs to get through this tough time, you'll be there for them and can provide resources to help.

Set an Appointment with the Family Doctor.

If you believe your teen is depressed, s/he should be screened by your family doctor for clinical depression. Your family doctor is familiar and less threatening to both you and your teen and can often have a conversation with your teen that you can't have. In addition, the doctor knows your child's history and will likely conduct a physical exam and some blood tests to make sure nothing else is happening physically.

See a Specialist.

If your doctor diagnoses your teen with depression, ask for a referral to a professional psychologist, psychiatrist or licensed clinical social worker for additional help. You and your teen will want to choose a professional who specialises in working with adolescents. Let your teenager be involved in choosing the specialist; not all professionals will connect with your teen.

Jointly develop a treatment plan.

You, your teen and the specialist will develop a treatment plan that will meet your teen's needs. The plan may involve therapy, counselling, medication and an exercise and diet regimen. As you visit with the specialist, before you leave make sure everyone understands what the treatment involves and what is expected to happen in the future.

Continue supporting your teen.

Just because your teen is now in therapy and/or on medication does not mean you can check out as a parent; stay involved. Regularly, check with your teen and see how things are going. Encourage your teen to stay physically and socially active. You might consider sharing that activity with the teen. A walk, run, bike ride or some hoops in the front driveway can be therapeutic for both of you. Be sure to remind him/her to take any prescribed medication.

Dealing with teenage depression can be a physical and emotional drain for any parent. However, identifying teen depression, working with medical professionals to develop a treatment approach, and consistently communicating and expressing love to your teen can make the process more productive for you and your teen and will help build his/her capacity to deal with life as it comes.

For support and information about suicide preven-tion, contact lifeline on 13 11 14 or suicide call back service on 1300 659 467.

What can parents do?

Many teens who commit or attempt suicide have given some type of warning to loved ones ahead of time. So, it's important for parents to know the warning signs so teens who might be suicidal can get the help they need.

Check their safety. If you're worried, don't leave them alone. Remove any means of suicide including weapons, medication, drugs, and alcohol – even access to the use of a car.

Some adults feel that kids who say they're going to hurt or kill themselves are 'just doing it for attention.' It's important to realise that if teens are ignored when seeking attention, it may increase the chance of them harming themselves (or even worse).

Getting attention in the form of Emergency Room visits, doctor's appointments, and residential treatment generally is not something teens want - unless they're seriously depressed and thinking about suicide or at least wishing they were dead. It's important to see warning signs as serious, not as 'attention-seeking behaviour' that should be ignored.

Keep a close eye on a teen who is depressed and withdrawn. Understanding depression in teens is very important since it can look different from commonly held beliefs about depression. For example, it may take the form of problems with friends, grades, sleep, or being cranky and irritable rather than chronic sadness or crying.

It's important to try to keep the lines of communication open and express your concern, support and love. If your teen confides in you, show that you take those concerns seriously. A fight with a friend might not seem like a big deal to you in the larger scheme of things, but for a teen it can feel immense and consuming. It's important not to minimise or discount what your teen is going through, as this can increase his/her sense of hopelessness.

If your teen doesn't feel comfortable talking with you, suggest a more neutral person, such as another relative, a clergy member, a coach, a school counsellor, or your child's doctor.

Some parents are reluctant to ask teens if they've been thinking about committing suicide or hurting themselves. Some fear that by asking - they will plant the idea of suicide in their teen's head.

It's always a good idea to ask, even though doing so can be difficult. Sometimes it helps to explain why you're asking. For instance, you might say: 'I've noticed that you've been talking a lot about wanting to be dead. Have you been having thoughts about trying to kill yourself?'

If you learn that your child is thinking about suicide, **get help immediately.** Your doctor can refer you to a psychologist or psychiatrist, or your local hospital's department of psychiatry can provide a list of doctors in your area. Your local mental health association or county medical society can also provide references.

If your teen is in a crisis, your local emergency room can conduct a comprehensive psychiatric evaluation and refer you to the appropriate resources. If you're unsure about whether you should bring your child to the emergency room, contact your doctor or the hospital staff.

Get help by calling Lifeline 13 11 14 or emergency services on 000 or you can take them to your local hospital emergency department.

If you've scheduled an appointment with a mental health professional, make sure to keep the appointment, even if your teen says s/he is feeling better or doesn't want to go. Suicidal thoughts do tend to come and go; however, it's important that your teen get help developing the skills necessary to decrease the likelihood that suicidal thoughts and behaviours will emerge again if a crisis arises.

If your teen refuses to go to the appointment, discuss this with the mental health professional - and consider attending the session and working with the clinician to make sure your teen has access to the help that's required. The counsellor also might be able to help you devise strategies to help your teen want to get help.

Remember that ongoing conflicts between a parent and child can fuel the fire for a teen who's feeling isolated, misunderstood, devalued, or suicidal. Get help to air family problems and resolve them in a constructive way. Also let the mental health professional know if there's a history of depression, substance abuse, family violence, or other stresses at home, such as an ongoing environment of criticism.

Helping teens cope with loss

What should you do if a family member, friend, or a classmate, has attempted or committed suicide? First, acknowledge your child's many emotions. Some teens say they feel guilty - especially those who felt they could have interpreted their friend's actions and words better.

Others say they feel angry with the person who committed or attempted suicide for having done something so selfish. Still others say they feel no strong emotions or don't know how to express how they feel. Reassure your child that there is no right or wrong way to feel, and that it's okay to talk about it when s/he feels ready.

When someone attempts suicide and survives, people might be afraid of or uncomfortable talking with him/her about it.

Tell your teen to resist this urge; this is the time when a person absolutely needs to feel connected to others.

Many schools address a student's suicide by calling in special counsellors to talk with the students and help them cope. If your teen is dealing with a friend or classmate's suicide, encourage him/her to make use of these resources or to talk to you or another trusted adult.

Teen suicide is preventable

Teen suicide is a growing health concern. It is the third-leading cause of death for young people ages fifteen to twenty-four, surpassed only by homicide and accidents. Causes of suicidal distress can be caused by psychological, environmental and social factors. Mental illness is the leading risk factor for suicide. Suicide risk-factors vary with age, gender, ethnic group, family dynamics and stressful life events.

Risk factors for suicide include depression and other mental disorders, and substance-abuse disorders (often in combination with other mental disorders). More than ninety percent of people who die by suicide have these risk factors.

The risk for suicide frequently occurs in combination with external circumstances that seem to overwhelm at-risk teens who are unable to cope with the challenges of adolescence because of predisposing vulnerabilities such as mental disorders. Examples of stressors are disciplinary problems, interpersonal losses, family violence, sexual orientation confusion, physical and sexual abuse and being the target of bullying.

In some situations, the suicidal person may refuse help and you can't force them to get help. You need to ensure the appropriate people are aware of the situation. Don't shoulder this responsibility by yourself.

Expressing emotional feelings

As children approach the teen years, they develop a better understanding of their feelings, and can better express their feelings to you.

When your child was younger, s/he may have become angry, but was unable to express why. As a teen, s/he should have learned how to express why s/he feels an emotion (positive or negative). This can keep you from having to constantly guess what his/her mood is or why s/he's grumpy, sad, depressed or extremely happy.

When dealing with angry teens, make sure you set limits on how they're allowed to express those feelings. Violent outbursts, physical aggression, and disrespectful behaviour should never be tolerated. Teach your teen how to manage his/her emotions without 'going off the rails.' Doing so will make their teen years much easier for both of you.

Predicting your teen's mood is practically impossible, but one thing's for sure: the most even-tempered teen will exhibit anger occasionally. Parents need to consider all the social, physical and emotional changes that are happening to their teen. It helps to know where their child is coming from and communication is the answer.

What causes teenage anger?

Between the ages of nine and thirteen, the typical teen must deal with an increased amount of homework, changing relationships with other boys and girls, of entering middle school where instead of being the oldest – they're now the youngest. They also need to deal with peer pressure to fit in.

Physically, teens change at a rapid pace. Their bodies grow, their hormones change, and their brains are developing. Unfortunately, many teens are not ready physically or emotionally to cope with all that's happening to them. They struggle to deal with all the changes in how they look, feel and are regarded by others. Angry feelings can be the result.

Teens may become angry at the slightest thing. A bad test grade may set them off, as may an argument with a friend, a bad day on the ball field, or a request to clean a bedroom.

Occasional outbursts are normal and are nothing to worry about. Keep in mind that when teens are angry, they want everyone to know it, so door slamming, pouting, and yelling are likely to happen.

If your teen hurts him/herself or others, or damages property, you should contact your paediatrician. Your child's doctor may recommend a trained professional who can help them deal with the upheaval they're going through.

- Offer suggestions that might help your teen calm down. If your teen's anger seems to be escalating, calmly suggest that s/he take some time in her room alone to calm down and pull him/herself together.
- Some teens find that journaling, drawing, or exercising helps them cope with stress, anger, and life's disappointments. Also, time alone with friends might help, as might a little television time or video game time.
- Allow your teen to vent, but not too much. It's great to blow off steam, but you also want to make sure that your teen doesn't fuel the fire and make him/herself even angrier.
- Ask your teen to consider how to prevent whatever it is that's bothering him/her. Is there any way for him/her to handle the situation positively or prevent it from happening again?
- Overlook small outbursts as they're quite normal and a part of growing up. Your job is to help your teen

develop coping skills so that s/he can improve the way s/he reacts to bad situations and disappointments.

Children's anger and your response

For normal anger outbursts, you can help your teen by:
- Remaining calm when your teen tries to talk to you. If you become angry that will only make his/her anger worse;
- Avoid offering suggestions at first, just let your teen talk it through, and keep from criticising or judging;
- Do say, 'I know you're angry, how can I help?' Don't say, 'This is no big deal. Forget about it.'
- Be sure your listening skills are up to the task. Don't interrupt your teen as s/he explains why s/he's upset. Ask questions to draw out more information and be sure to keep your voice very, very calm;
- Keep in mind that your teen may not really be angry. S/he may be disappointed, jealous, embarrassed, or scared. S/he just may not know how to properly react to the situation s/he's facing, so anger is the result. Helping teens to identify their emotions is a good first step towards helping them learn how to cope with them;
- Make sure your teen is getting enough sleep. A sleep-deprived child will get angry more often, just because s/he's tired and can't cope.
   It doesn't matter if it's the school year or the summer months, many teens just aren't getting the sleep they need. For many children sleep isn't a priority, but even though your teen is getting older, s/he still needs to rest. It's recommended that pre-teens get at least nine hours of sleep a night, but busy teens often fall short on fulfilling that amount. Schedules, homework, sleepovers, television, texting and computer time are usually the culprits.

Getting a good night's sleep

Here's what you need to know about sleep, and the obstacles teens face when it comes to getting a good night's rest.

1. Quit caffeine:
Sleep, children and caffeine just don't mix. Caffeine should be avoided as much as possible after three o'clock. Children who consume iced tea, caffeine drinks, coffee or other caffeinated beverages may pay the price later that night. Even foods such as chocolate or coffee ice cream might have small traces of caffeine and should be avoided after three o'clock.

2. Quiet time:
Sometimes it's hard for teens to transition from a hectic day to bedtime. Make sure your teen's curfew allows him/her time to get ready for bed and relax a little at home before laying down to rest. You can also help children sleep by offering suggestions that will help them calm down and begin the process of rest. Television and computers should be off limits, an hour or so before your teen's ideal bedtime hour. Before they go to sleep, children can participate in activities that help them relax, such as reading a book or taking a warm shower.

3. Stop snacking:
It's hard to get a teen to stop snacking but eating right before bedtime is never a good idea. During the day, make sure your teen has plenty of healthy snacks to choose from so that you know his/her growing body is getting the nutrition it needs, and that s/he's not loaded up with sugar, which can also make sleeping difficult.

4. **Kill the light**:
Toddlers often need a night light on to get to sleep. However, night lights for teens can disrupt changing hormone levels and interfere with a good night's rest. This includes leaving their computer screens on. If they have left

the internet on – each e-mail they receive will likely result in a computer sound to announce its arrival. This little noise is enough to keep the teen awake most of the night. Before they go to sleep, teens must be encouraged to turn off any phone, music, television or computer screens in their rooms.

5. Slow down:
If your teen is truly struggling with bedtime and has troubling waking up in the morning, take a serious look at the family schedule. Teens who are overbooked with activities may need to slow down a little, in order to develop a regular sleep schedule.

6. Children, sleep and stress:
Stress can interfere with a child's sleep, just as it can with an adult's sleep. School problems, friend problems, bullying problems or problems at home might be what's keeping your teen up at night. Encourage your teens to talk about these stressors and help them deal with them.

Chapter 8
Growing Up

Button Battery Dangers

Button batteries found in remote controls and other household electronic devices are a severe and little-known risk for young children and pets. They're found in many common devices: bathroom scales; reading lights; flameless candles; games and toys; watches; calculators; torches and laser lights; remote control devices that unlock car doors, garage doors and control MP3 speakers; musical greeting cards and hearing aids. They present a problem whether they're ingested or inserted in an ear or nose; wherever they have prolonged contact with the body and particularly in moist parts of the body like their ears or stomach.

Damage occurs when the battery charge generates a chemical reaction that causes a localised caustic injury. It's vital to detect a swallowed battery as soon as possible because of the nature of the threat involved. While most other ingested foreign objects will pass through the gastrointestinal tract without causing any concerns, button batteries (depending on their size) tend to lodge in the oesophagus or food pipe. Once stuck, damage starts to occur after one or two hours.

If the ingestion has not been recognised, the battery could erode through into vital organs, causing catastrophic damage and possibly death. If parents or owners of a pet believe a battery could have been swallowed, they must seek medical attention immediately and not give any food or water.

One of the greatest risks is when parents are changing or discarding batteries that have gone flat. Don't leave new or flat batteries within reach of children or pets. Flat or dead batteries still contain enough life to generate an electrical current once ingested.

There are many signs that point to ingesting a battery such as: chest pain, coughing, nausea, vomiting (especially if it has blood in it) and abdominal pain or diarrhoea and fever.

The coin-sized lithium button batteries can lodge in the throats of children, where saliva immediately triggers an electrical current, causing a chemical reaction that can severely burn through the oesophagus in as little as two hours. An estimated four children per week in Canada present to an emergency department with a button battery related injury.

A significant problem arises when the parent doesn't know that their child has ingested or inserted a button battery. This is particularly so for children under the age of three, who are more likely to ingest a foreign body and not be able to tell someone about it. Unfortunately, symptoms can mimic common childhood conditions, with vomiting, drooling and cough.

The following article was in an Australian paper:

'On June 30th, 2013 four-year-old Summer Steer went into cardiac arrest and died after ingesting a 2cm button battery that lodged in her esophagus.

Her mother, Andrea Shoesmith had already taken her to their Tewantin GP at least twice prior to her hospital visits. Summer had been complaining of a stomach ache, had a temperature and her mother had started noticing 'black poos'. Their doctor advised that Summer had a stomach bug and sent her home. It has now been determined that the battery must have been ingested before she saw her GP.

The night before she died, Summer had been vomiting blood with symptoms including a sore stomach, black bowel movements and a temperature. She was taken by ambulance around midnight to the Noosa Hospital emergency ward and was discharged after seeing a doctor for around fifteen minutes.

Her mother said, 'The doctor said it was normal – that she had a nose bleed and swallowed the blood and vomited it up. I thought she was dying.'

But when Summer vomited 'bright red blood' outside the front doors of the Emergency Department, the doctor scooped her up and put her under observation.

The four-year-old was discharged the following morning at 6:15 am with a diagnosis of epistaxis (nosebleed). She was given a bag for vomiting and a tablet to control it.

Within an hour, however, Summer was rushed back to hospital after her mother said that Summer got up and vomited bright red blood and then collapsed again.

She was re-admitted to the hospital. By the time an x-ray was finally done that uncovered the battery and she was airlifted to Brisbane - it was too late. Bleeding heavily from the mouth and nose, Summer went into cardiac arrest and was pronounced dead on June 30th.

She was the first child in Australia to die from swallowing a lithium battery although a pre-inquest hearing revealed around 260 children swallow lithium batteries each year. In Australia four cases a week are diagnosed. The chemical reaction is triggered by the body's saliva and can keep burning through various layers of tissue organs right through to the spine.'

Several years later a man decided he would sue McDonald's for allegedly serving him a hamburger containing a button battery. He was half way through the burger when he started choking. He felt something hard in the back of his throat and coughed vigorously. His wife rushed him to hospital, and he felt whatever it was go down and he had instant relief. They did tests and kept him under observation.

By the next morning he was in agony. The doctors thought it might be a button battery, so he had an endoscopy, X-rays and three colonoscopies before the device could be removed. He was on morphine for days and still must take medication for gastric ulcers.

He has launched legal proceedings against McDonald's seeking compensation for the pain and suffering and for any future medical expenses he might have. He's also suing for lost income. At this point McDonalds have not taken responsibility for the battery being in the burger. Investigations are pending.

So, it's not only children who could swallow these dangerous batteries and everyone must be careful about how they store or dispose of all button batteries.

Trust

Parents need to start gaining their children's trust early in their lives. Children need their parents' trust to feel loved, but this trust can often break down during their teen years. Teens (who so far, couldn't wait to tell their parents everything) may suddenly clam up. This causes their parents to start imagining the worst: they're on drugs, they were drinking at a party or having sex with their partners. Often the more invasive the parents' questions become, the less the teens reveal.

Don't pry. Let your teenagers have their privacy except in issues that are important. Make sure they understand the concept of 'consequences of their actions.' For instance, *'I don't want to force you to study, but I feel it's important to me as a parent to limit the time you spend watching TV until your grades improve.'*

Parents should explain why they need the information they ask for and share their disappointment when their teenagers break their trust. When teens feel their parents are trusting (not controlling) they'll volunteer information themselves.

If you have pre-teen children, now is the time to consider the following questions and come up with a plan of action satisfactory to both parents. This will prepare you for what you'd do in these situations and give some continuity to your actions should the need occur. If you haven't considered the following questions, think about them now, get your spouse's opinion and see how you'd want to deal with them:

1. What would you say to your daughter or son if you didn't approve of their choice of date?
2. How would you set dating rules (week nights, weekends, curfew)?
3. Would you allow their girlfriend or boyfriend to study with them in their bedroom?
4. When do you think their sex education should begin? Would you do this by giving them books on the topic? How would you broach the topic and what would you say to them? How far would you go in your explanations? At what age?
5. How and when would you talk to them about their own sexuality? With your daughter? Your son? Would you be as cautious and informative to both your daughters and your sons?
6. When would you discuss pre-marital sex, contraception and sexually transmitted diseases?
7. What would you do if your fifteen-year-old daughter told you that she was pregnant? What would you say to her? How would you feel about the father of her child? What would you advise her to do about her pregnancy or would you leave it up to her? Are you informed enough about the choices available to her? Would you support your daughter, no matter what choice she made?

8. How would this differ if it were your son who told you that his girlfriend was pregnant? How would you feel about his girlfriend? What would you advise him to do?

Relatively few people abuse hard drugs compared to the number of those that abuse soft drugs. Help your teen learn how to say *'No'* to alcohol and drugs. Make sure they know they can turn to you if they've been exposed to the drug culture. If approached, your teen should ignore the person, walk away or repeat *'No'* repeatedly like a broken record.

Many police forces are going into the schools. Police officers have on-the-job exposure and have been on drug busts, so can relate personal stories that hit home with their audiences. This makes drug and alcohol problems more real to children. They learn what drugs look like and understand what makes a drug 'an upper' or 'a downer.' Show your endorsement of those programs by offering your assistance and support.

Some teenagers breeze through their teen years with only minimal disruption to themselves and their parents. But others, because they have so much trouble understanding themselves, have difficulty understanding their parents as well. Some do things intentionally to annoy their parents. Their negative behaviour includes lying, defying authority figures, leaving their belongings lying around and playing truant from school.

Hard being a teenager

I'm glad I'm not a teenager right now. Drug and alcohol peddlers tempt them. They see members of their peer group smoking, drinking and taking drugs and many have been enticed into 'just trying it,' then find themselves hooked into an addictive habit.

At school, students are often inundated with nothing but negatives. They seldom hear from their parents and teachers about what they've done right, but they certainly hear about what they've done wrong.

Teens are far more upset by their parent's fighting than they let on. Some miss the opportunity of observing loving, nurturing parents who care deeply for each other. Without this daily exposure of how men and women can work together in harmony, they don't learn how to get along in romantic relationships of their own.

A large proportion of teens these days are living in broken homes and their parents have less time to spend with them. The absent parent often makes up for the time they don't spend with them by lavishing expensive gifts on them. When asked what they want from their parents, many teens would say, to spend more time with their respective parents.

Added to this, are the financial worries of a single-parent home. Teens fear they won't have enough money to do everything in life they hope to do. Often, an immediate need for money for education is a prime source of stress.

Others see both their parents working to keep up with the cost of living and face the frustration of realising that unless they have a good education, they too will be doomed to a low-paying job. They see university and college entrance requirements raised higher and higher along with their costs. For many, no matter how hard they work, they can't see themselves being able to meet the minimum requirements. Parents should encourage them to do the best they can and if necessary, obtain private tutoring.

Another focus of teenagers is their environment. They see the mess their parents, grandparents and ancestors have made of their universe and have concerns about the quality of the water, air and food they eat and how their world will be during their adulthood.

Family conferences

Whenever there's an important issue that involves the entire family; call a family conference. This could be when Mom goes back to work, when Dad gets a promotion and must move to another city, when a relative is very ill and may die or any other important family issue. Family conferences are held to discuss problems within the family, to delegate new responsibilities and to touch base with how family members are doing in their lives.

To prepare for a family conference about delegation of tasks, a parent would write down all the chores that need completion around the home and yard (include *all* tasks). Copies of this list are made for each member of the family who's old enough to read. Then a family conference is held:

1. At the family conference, all members are expected to volunteer for some of the chores. Then, the parents fill in the chores they feel comfortable handling.
2. The remaining tasks are then assigned. All members are free to negotiate and trade chores with an accepting member. Each person must know how and when s/he's expected to complete his/her duties.
3. Anyone trying a new task receives training. One parent asks each family member, *'Can I count on you to do these chores competently and on time?'* Parents are to wait until they receive a verbal commitment from each family member.
4. Parents also explain that they don't want to have to nag anyone to complete his or her chores properly.
5. Then, one parent follows-up, to make sure the allotted tasks are completed properly.

If you've received the excuse, *'I don't have time,'* help them plan their time. Try to avoid power struggles. If one teenager or child has the job of taking out the garbage, another must clean the bathroom (including the toilet) another mows the lawn, etc. Start job rotation to guarantee completion of distasteful chores.

To make sure this process works, make sure you give rewards to your children - signs of love and appreciation. Acknowledge jobs well done, by arranging special family treats for exceptional work or anything above and beyond the call of duty.

Out of control teens

As one father lamented, *'My sixteen-year-old son has been acting very aggressively lately. He shouts at his sister, his friends and is disrespectful of adults. He's also started throwing things around when he's mad. He's out of control. How can I deal with his disruptive behaviour?'*

Find your nearest Tough Love group and attend a meeting. Parents can examine the following criteria to find out if they need the help of Tough Love. The key to the Tough Love approach is letting children be responsible for their own behaviour and the consequences of that behaviour. Assess your situation by checking any items in the following lists that describe your situation:

Your teenager has run away:
- Overnight;
- For two days;
- For a week;
- For more than a week.

Your teenager has:
- Missed dinner;
- Been late;
- Been stoned or drunk;

- Didn't come home at all;
  - Overnight;
  - For two days;
  - For a week;
  - For more than a week.

At Home:
- You and your spouse argue about your teenager's behaviour;
- You have withdrawn from your spouse;
- Your spouse has withdrawn from you;
- You have not had a peaceful night's sleep;
- You hate to hear the phone ring when your teenager is not home;
- You or your spouse has lost time from work because of your teenager.

At school, your teenager has been:
- Tardy;
- Absent;
- Playing hooky;
- Suspended;
- You've been called by the school for bad behaviour.

Your teenager has been violent:
- Verbally;
- Physically to the house or furniture;
- Physically to you, your spouse or your children;
- Physically to other people;
  - In school;
  - With the police.

Legally, your teenager has:
- Received summons;
- Received fines;

- Received tickets;
- Been involved in accidents;
- Been charged with drug incidents;
- Been charged with drinking;
- Been arrested.

If you've checked two areas in the school category, two areas in the home category and one area in the legal category, the crisis is building. If you've checked more areas, you're already in crisis and should contact your local Tough Love group for help. They can help when parents have tried everything else from police to social services and find traditional methods don't work. Do it now, your family's future depends upon it.

Many community and counselling programs help troubled teens. If you find your teen is not responding to your efforts to help, call in professional re-enforcement. One community program that's been successful, pairs a model student with a teen in trouble. Trained counsellors monitor the teens' progress. The volunteer model student provides anything from help with homework, to companionship and a shoulder to cry on.

Today it often seems that the children have all the rights. Tough Love groups advocate that parents have rights too. This organisation has helped many parents who have incorrigible teens. It's a support group for parents. These groups are not there to blame anyone, because at this point, it doesn't matter what caused the problem. The issue is - how to solve the situation.

Parents need to set a 'Bottom Line' - something they want to accomplish with their teenager. It might be something as simple as insisting they take out the garbage, clean their room or use headphones when they play their music.

You can find your local Tough Love group by going to www.toughlove.org.au/findgroups.htm

Teamwork

One valuable skill teens learn through competitive team sports, is how to co-operate with their peers. This co-operation often stops at the end of the school ground. Many teens come home, do little or nothing to help around the home, but have plenty of time to get into trouble.

In many homes both parents or in a single parent home, the sole parent works full-time away from the home. Their children and teenagers often complain that their parents have no time for them. Their stressed out, hard pressed parents are advised to use the energy of their teens to help with the smooth running of their home. This way, the parents have more time for family activities. Parents would initiate this by calling a family conference and allotting tasks to those old enough to do them.

Puberty:

What is puberty? Has your teen asked that question yet? If not, s/he probably will at some point. Puberty is the time of life when a child's body transitions into an adult body. The process takes several years and can be a difficult time for both the child and the parent. You might use a caterpillar; cocoon then butterfly as an example. The child is the caterpillar – the teen is the cocoon where changes happen, and the butterfly is the finished adult product. Going through those stages can be frightening and difficult for some individuals.

There are many stages of puberty for both boys and girls. Parents can help their child adjust to puberty and make the most of the transition to adulthood.

Puberty for boys:

At some point during the teen years, a boy may begin to experience the stages of puberty. The relationship between boys and puberty can be complicated for both the child and his parents. Knowing what to look for can ease your mind and help your teen through these enormous physical and emotional changes.

Below are some of the more typical signs of puberty in boys. Keep in mind that these stages may appear gradually, and it may take several years for your child to completely cycle through all the phases of puberty.

In general, boys begin puberty at some point between the ages of nine and fourteen.

Physical changes in boys
- Growth spurts;
- Appearance of facial hair;
- Broadening of shoulder muscles;
- Development of chest muscles;
- Body odour;
- Pimples or facial breakouts;
- Hair growth in pubic and underarm areas;
- Growth of testicles;
- Erections or wet dreams;
- Deepening of the voice, although this is more likely in the later stages of puberty.

Emotional changes in boys
- Interest in the opposite sex;
- Mood changes;
- Anxiety or excitement about the changes he's going through;

- Less talkative and open with parents especially discussing how he feels;
- Shyness, nervousness around girls, or can be flirtatious with girls.

Puberty for Girls

Girls begin puberty between the ages of eight and twelve. Knowing what to look for can ease your mind and help your teen through these enormous physical and emotional changes. While some of the signs of puberty may take a while to develop, others may appear as if they happened overnight.

Below are some of the more typical signs of puberty in girls. Keep in mind that these stages may appear gradually, and it may take three to four years for your child to cycle through all the phases of puberty. Share these signs with your teen daughter, so she knows what to expect. One of the first signs of puberty in a girl is that she complains that her chest hurts as little breasts start to form.

Be sure you explain how she might handle her first period if you're not around to help, such as when she's at school or away from home. Here's how to prepare her:

To start, talk with your daughter about what to expect when her period begins. Explain some of the common changes a girl might experience before her period starts such as cramps, headaches, a lack of energy, a feeling of wetness on her underpants, etc. Also, take the time to show her how to properly use a pad, so that if you're not there, she'll know what to do.

Explain to your child that if she thinks her period has arrived, she needs to ask for permission to go to the girls' bathroom to check. (It's a good idea for all teen girls to keep a pad in their book bags or school lockers, just in case. A small pad can easily fit into a change purse, or a small handbag.) If your daughter doesn't have a pad, instruct her to go the school nurse right away. The nurse will be able to provide her with one. Some schools have sanitary napkin machines in the rest rooms but warn her not to rely on them having supplies or she might not have the coins required to buy one.

Period strategy: Think ahead

If your teen daughter is headed to camp or somewhere else for an extended time, you'll need to think ahead. Pack a few pads in her suitcase. Give her a letter to give to her counsellor should she get her first period while she's away. The letter should explain the situation, as well as other information her counsellor might need to know about her.

Make sure your daughter understands that she is to give the letter to her counsellor only if her first period comes. Also, explain to your daughter that if her first period comes while she's at camp, she may need to abstain from swimming until her flow has ended.

Be sure your daughter is well informed about menstruation and the normal changes of puberty. There are many wonderful resources available today that truly help girls through these changes in positive ways. In addition, if you help your daughter learn to track her period once she's begun to menstruate, that will help ease her stress and anxiety a little and help her know when to be alert for her period starting.

By prepping your daughter, she'll know that there is no reason to worry about when her period will begin, because when it does begin, she'll be ready.

Physical changes in girls
- Growth spurts. (Girls are often taller than boys their age at this stage);
- Body shape changes as body fat accumulates around the hips and thighs, giving girls a curvier shape;
- Breast development;
- Body odour and skin breakouts due to increased oil gland production;
- Hair growth in the underarm area, on the legs and in the pubic area;
- Menstruation begins, typically around the age of twelve.

Emotional changes in girls
- Mood swings may begin, punctuated with bouts of anger, sadness and other emotional fluctuations;
- Romantic feelings and interest in the opposite sex – but boys their age are often shorter, so they may gravitate towards older boys;
- Anxiety and/or excitement about the changes they're going through;
- Concerns over increased responsibility, fitting in socially and separating from their parents.

Teen girls may become self-conscious

A major part of emotional development is self-awareness. As your teen becomes more aware of herself and the world around her, she may become self-conscious about her appearance, her clothes, and just about everything else. During the teen years girls often compare themselves with their peers and with the images they see in magazines, on television and in the movies. Unfortunately, many girls believe that they aren't as talented, pretty, smart or likable as other girls.

During the teen years, girls need gentle reassurance that there's nothing wrong with them, and that they're developing the way they're meant to. Explain that they're a work in progress and are just going through the stages required for them to become a woman. Offer your love and support and ask how you can help them deal with issues they might be struggling with. Also, be aware of the signs of eating disorders, as well as the symptoms of depression.

Emotional development and reasoning

As your child grows s/he may show signs of sophisticated reasoning, another major milestone in your child's emotional development. As your child thinks more and more like an adult, it makes communicating with him/her a little easier and a little harder.

The more your child understands, the easier it is to make your point and hopefully, get it across to him/her. However, teens are famous for trying to negotiate with their parents or for finding inconsistencies in their parents' reasoning that they can use against them. Expect your teen to challenge you and the decisions you make from time to time.

Be sure to manage your own emotions when your teen is pushing your buttons. Be sure you take a time-out for yourself when you think you might be 'losing it.'

Also, it's okay to take time to think about how you want to respond to your teen when s/he has challenged your authority or presented a side to an issue that you hadn't considered. You could say, 'It's clear that this is a complicated matter. I need time to think about this and after I do, we'll talk about it again.'

Emotional development and romantic feelings

Teens may begin to show a romantic interest in others even as young as age nine. Generally, teens aren't mature enough to handle dating, but they may talk about dating, who they want to date and mention classmates who are already dating.

You don't want to forbid your teen to date, because that will only encourage your child to rebel against you. Allow your teen to mix with members of the opposite sex *in groups* (if they're close in age). It's fine to allow your teen to think about dating, but don't encourage dating until your child is ready for the experience around thirteen or fourteen.

Chapter 9
Entering Middle School

Starting Middle School

Starting middle school can be daunting for some teens. To help your child adjust, begin discussing the types of changes s/he can expect long before that first day of class. Take your time and be there to answer any questions your child might have.

If your teen is like most, s/he's probably feeling a mix of excitement and apprehension at the prospect of beginning middle school. They will be going from being the oldest students in a school to being the youngest. Helping teens make the transition from elementary school to middle school helps prepare them for a successful academic year. While it may be difficult for you or your teen to say goodbye to elementary school, the middle school years provide plenty of opportunities for your son or daughter to develop socially, academically, and intellectually.

To get them off on the right foot, consider the following pointers.

Discuss Changes

Make sure your teens understand that middle school may be very different from elementary school. Help them understand that their teachers will expect them to be more responsible and take on additional homework. Lockers, gym class, mandatory showers after gym, multiple teachers and a whole new group of kids may just be a few of your child's new experiences. In addition, teens will be responsible for finding their new classrooms and arriving on time for each class.

On the upside, point out that middle school will offer social activities and clubs that elementary schools never had, such as band, sports clubs and other opportunities. Also, many middle school cafeterias offer items such as a salad bar, potato bar, or a pizza bar. Find out what your child's school offers in terms of extra-curricular activities, as well as elective classes. Accentuate the positive!

Below are a few steps you can take to prepare your child for the challenges and benefits of middle school.

1. Talk about the upside of Middle School

The idea of moving up to middle school can be scary for some children. But middle school offers many benefits and opportunities. Talk to your teen about all the organisations and clubs s/he'll be able to join, as well as the independence that comes with being a pre-teen. Point out other opportunities the school offers and encourage him/her to become involved right away, when everyone in his/her class is just as new to the school as s/he is.

Starting middle school is a transition for any teen. Gone are the comfortable elementary years where they enjoyed recess. They now change rooms to attend the classes on different subjects. There'll be an increased amount of homework and they will be given more responsibility and will be expected to get things done. To help your children prepare for the changes they will face in middle school, be sure to concentrate on all the wonderful benefits they'll enjoy as well.

They will have:

- The chance to take electives such as sports, band, music, or art;
- The opportunity to participate in after-school clubs or the middle school student government;

- Their own locker to decorate and personalise;
- The chance to meet and make new friends;
- A variety of teachers with different teaching styles;
- A few minutes of down time between classes;
- More menu choices at the school cafeteria;
- The knowledge that all the other students will be starting new just like them.

They will have the opportunity of:

- Being treated more like an adult and less like a kid;
- Trying out for school plays, school teams, or cheerleading squads;
- Taking a foreign language for the first time;
- Getting out of school earlier in the day;
- Going to school dances.

2. Address your child's fears about middle school

Many teens may worry about finding their classes, opening their lockers, or dressing for gym class. Tackle your child's fears as they occur and point out that everyone in his/her class is new to the school and the school rules. Also, point out that many of his/her fears will be addressed at an open house or school orientation either before or soon after school starts. Be sure your child attends because s/he'll learn the layout of the school, important rules and procedures, and where his/her classes will be located.

Discuss his/her schedule so s/he has an idea of how long it will take to get from one class to another. Keep in mind that s/he may need to use a washroom or stop for a drink at the drinking fountain. If your child misses the orientation, or if the middle school doesn't offer one, call the principal and ask for a tour of the middle school during the summer months.

In the meantime, spend a little time showing your teen how to use a locker combination and offer tips on getting to his/her classes on time.

Once teens have their new classroom schedule, help them organise their belongings so they know what they'll need to bring with them between visits to their lockers.

Explain that they should avoid chit-chatting with friends in-between classes which might make them late.

Finally, reassure them that they'll feel more comfortable at their new school in just a few weeks.

3. Prepare Your Teen for Changes

Be sure you go over other changes that your teen is likely to encounter such as peer pressure, increased homework, making new friends, getting involved in clubs or activities, and increased responsibilities at home. Your teen will likely encounter new school rules when s/he begins middle school. What should s/he do if s/he breaks one of them accidentally? How should s/he react?

4. Help with Homework

Homework during the middle school years tends to increase and parents can often find themselves unable to help with specific subjects. But parents can still do quite a lot to help their children tackle homework assignments and complete class projects. Tricks include setting up an environment that helps your teen concentrate on homework in order to complete it quickly. It's also important to keep a family calendar to track special assignments and projects and keep your teen organised.

5. Take a Tour of the Middle School

Touring your child's school, either together or separately, is a wonderful way to answer any questions your teen might have about middle school and ease any anxieties. A tour will show your child where s/he can find all the places s/he'll have to go in the day (gym, cafeteria, locker, etc.) and that will give him/her a sense of confidence on his/her first day.

6. Consider Resources about Middle School

There are several books on the market that can prepare your child for the adjustments of middle school. Some are very specific, written exclusively for teen boys or teen girls. It's not a bad idea to make an investment in one of these resources. They may even help you better understand some of the challenges your child will face, and that can help you help your teen.

Some of those for girls are:
- A Smart Girl's Guide to Starting Middle School;
- A Smart Girl's Guide to Boys;
- A Smart Girl's Guide to Friendship Troubles;
- A Smart Girl's Guide to Sticky Situations, and
- A Smart Girl's Guide to Manners.

All authored by Julie Williams.

How to make the transition easier

Get Organised:

The first step is to prepare for the day ahead of time. Be sure your child knows that before s/he goes to bed his/her:
- homework needs to be finished;
- clothes for the next day should be chosen;
- lunch made; and

- book bag and shoes waiting for him/her at the front door.

Also, be sure they have a working alarm clock, and make sure they set it so that they have enough time in the morning to eat and get ready for school. This is their responsibility - you should not be responsible for ensuring they get up on time. By being prepared and ready to go when they wake up, they'll minimise problems that could occur. They'll also be more likely to catch the bus on time and missing the school bus is an easy way to get the school day off on the wrong foot.

Encourage Strong Friendships:

School students face a lot of social issues while at school, including bullying and social exclusion. Be sure your child takes the time to develop strong friendships, which can help if your child runs into trouble on the bus or at school. Friendships also help your child deal with teacher issues, homework problems and other teen concerns.

Being excluded from a group can have devastating effects, up to and including suicide.

Teaching Independence to Your Teen

You may want to begin giving your teens a little independence once they start middle school. For many families it's during the middle school years that children may be left home alone for the first time. This milestone should be approached carefully and with much consideration and preparation. Take time to transition your teens from constantly being supervised to being home alone. Be sure to check-up on them periodically to make sure they're safe and using their time alone wisely.

They should be encouraged to be part of the family team and take over some of the chores their parents have done in the past. For instance, because the teen will likely get home before the parents, have both your sons and daughters take steps to start with the preparation for dinner. One could set the table; another could peel the vegetables, and another could make a salad or simple desert.

Call a family conference with your children and instruct them how they can participate as part of the team – their family:

How to make a bed:

Many toddlers can make their beds quite well, but you'd be surprised how many pre-teens have either 'forgotten' or never learned in the first place. Ask your children to make their bed every day before school. Also, teach them how to remove the sheets for washing and replace them later. Making their own bed is something any pre-teen can do. On the weekends, they should be responsible for cleaning their rooms, vacuuming the carpets which might may also motive them to pick up the clutter in their rooms.

How to make a simple meal:

By the time your children are teens, they should be able to make a simple meal. It could be a salad, a sandwich or maybe just a can of ravioli or soup. Your children should know all the safety rules, especially if they're using the microwave or oven, which can pose certain hazards. If you're uncomfortable with your children cooking - teach them how to make a peanut butter and jelly sandwich or a healthy salad.

How to contribute to the family:

Teens should be contributing to family chores. Chores your child can do could include cleaning the bathroom they use, feeding pets, loading and emptying the dishwasher, sweeping the front porch or vacuuming. Your child may also be able to do laundry (supervised). Teach them how to sort clothes by colour, load the machine, add detergent and work the dryer. Once your children have mastered one chore, teach them another to expand their growing skill set.

How to prioritise:

Your teens probably can't prioritise like you can, but they should be able to master basic prioritising, such as: should they work on their science project that's due tomorrow, or should they watch television. Of course, you can't expect your children to think like an adult, but you should notice growth regarding prioritising and taking responsibility for certain aspects of their lives.

How to call for help in an emergency:

Emergencies can happen at any time, so it's important your children know how to respond should something go wrong, and you're not there. Teens should know how to contact you, a trusted neighbour as well as how to call emergency services 000.

How to pick up after him/herself:

Your children should have been taught to clean up after themselves before they start pre-school. If your teens are leaving their clothes on the floor, their dinner plate on the table and their toothbrush in the sink, it's catch-up time.

In fact, your children are old enough now to not only pick-up after themselves, but also old enough to help you pick-up other things around the home. Encourage your teens to clear the dinner table after meals and tidy the TV room before and after friends come over.

Practice basic hygiene:

By now your teens should have hygiene basics down to a science. They should be brushing their teeth morning and night without being asked. They should also be washing their face and brushing their hair without your having to remind them. You may still need to encourage then to shower and use deodorant, but they'll have that down pat before long if you persist.

Discuss the Middle School Rules:

If your middle schooler tends to find out about rules the hard way, save him/her a little time by going over the school's dress code, cell phone rules, bus rules, and cafeteria rules. Discuss the school's consequence policy (and yours, too).

Talk About Social Pressures:

The middle school years present enormous social pressures for children and introduces them to a variety of dangers. Take every possible opportunity to reinforce your family's rules and values regarding smoking, drugs, alcohol, dating, co-ed sleepovers and any other issues or concerns.

Role play with your children about how they should react when confronted by a classmate who wants them to smoke or drink alcohol. Stay on top of your children's social situation by getting to know their friends and their parents. If you see a change in your children's personality, or their grades begin to drop, act. Contact the school guidance counsellor to find out if there might be something going on at school or on the bus, such as bullying. Remind your children every now and then that you're there to help, and that they can talk to you about anything.

Ask About Concerns:

Be sure to give your children numerous opportunities to ask questions about their new experience and express concerns. You may think your daughter is stressed about changing classes, when she may really be worried about whether she'll remember her locker combination.

Assess Your Child's Skills and Abilities:

Starting all over at a new school is hard enough but starting over when you're struggling with math or reading can make the experience a nightmare. Consider tutoring services if your child's academic skills aren't where they should be. Also, ask the middle school about any resources they may provide to help your child succeed academically.

Conclusion

As parents, I hope you took this information to heart and will be better informed on what you can do to help your teens and pre-teens make it through the minefield they'll be stepping into.

I've always believed that the first five years of a child's life are the most important. Those are the years where they learn about life; what's right and what's wrong. So, start out right, and spend quality time with your children, no matter how old they are. Teach them not to bully others and how to deal with a bully and not become targets.

Communication is the answer. Asking the right questions and letting your children know that you're there for them; that you'll love them no matter what they do - is the way to go. At first, they might balk at this, but if you persist, they will slowly, but surely come around.

Bibliography

Roberta Cava	***Dealing with Difficult Spouses and Children;*** Cava Consulting, 2013
	Dealing with School Bullying – Society's Educational Disgrace; Cava Consulting, 2013
Jo Frost	***Supernanny – How to get the best from your children;*** Kingswell Pub. 2005
Julie Williams Montalbano	***Smart Girl's Guide to Manners;*** American Girl, 2004
	A Smart Girl's Guide to Starting Middle School; American Girl, 2004
	A Smart Girl's Guide to Friendship Troubles; American Girl, 2013
Nancy Hoyoke & Bonnie Timmons	***A Smart Girl's Guide to Boys;*** American Girl, 2001
	A Smart Girl's Guide to Sticky, Icky Situations; American Girl, 2002
Frank C Hawkins	***The Boy's Body Guide;*** Boy's Guide Books
Gary J. Campbell & Frank C Hawkins	***Boy's Guide 2 Girls;*** 2012
Joseph Connolly	***Boys & Girls;*** Quercus Pub. 2015
Kate Gruenwald	***Boy's Guide to Becoming a Teen;***

Pfeifer	American Medical Assn. 2006
Marilyn Mairs Saunders	***Growing up Smart;*** Amazon Books, 2015
Irene Keller	***Benjamin Rabbit and the Stranger Danger;*** Littlehampton Book Services Ltd, 1985
Raffi Cavoukian	***Lightweb; Darkweb – Three reasons to reform social media be4 it reforms us;*** Homeland Press, 2013

www.ingramcontent.com/pod-product-compliance
Lightning Source LLC
LaVergne TN
LVHW051559070426
835507LV00021B/2656